POWER IN
PREACHING

W. E. SANGSTER

POWER IN
PREACHING

ABINGDON PRESS

NEW YORK   NASHVILLE

POWER IN PREACHING

© *The Epworth Press 1958*

Library of Congress Catalog Card Number: 58-10462

SET UP, PRINTED, AND BOUND BY THE
PARTHENON PRESS, AT NASHVILLE,
TENNESSEE, UNITED STATES OF AMERICA

To Ella Florence Fondren

whose Lecture Foundation
first took me to
SOUTHERN METHODIST UNIVERSITY
Dallas

and whose dedicated life
is a challenge to many

PREFACE

This book contains the thirty-ninth series of Fondren Lectures given at Southern Methodist University, Dallas, Texas.

I shall not soon forget the cordial welcome given me by the students and faculty of Perkins School of Theology and by the officers of the university. Texas—large in so many ways—is largest of all in the spontaneity and warmth and sincerity of the welcome it gives to a stranger in the midst. Indeed, I have ceased to be a stranger and been adopted as a son! I offer these lectures—though all unworthy—as a mark of my affection for my "other mother."

I wish to thank my son-in-law, the Rev. C. Dennis Phippen, M.A., and my friend, the Rev. Greville P. Lewis, B.A., B.D., for reading the typescript and making helpful comments.

W. E. SANGSTER

CONTENTS

"Go ye into all the world, and preach the gospel to the whole creation."—*Jesus*

"I charge thee in the sight of God, and of Christ Jesus, who shall judge the quick and the dead, . . . preach the word; be instant in season, out of season; reprove, rebuke, exhort, with all longsuffering and teaching."—*Paul*

1

BELIEVE IN IT

If a man committed to the high task of proclaiming the gospel was to pose the question to his own mind, "How does power come into preaching?" he might begin to think (1) of the techniques of sermon making—of arresting beginnings, firm structures, and clean conclusions; or (2) of the deep spiritualities of the preacher's calling and of the way in which a man may keep himself open to the inflow of the Holy Spirit and make himself, in ways beyond exact analysis, a messenger of God; or (3) of the broad hinterland of his own nature which lies beyond both these realms, where faith really keeps her castle in his soul—faith in the gospel itself and faith in preaching as the means of its proclamation —without which any preacher becomes a charlatan.

Each of those categories has a contribution to make to the complete answer to the question. Power in preaching involves—in varying degrees of importance—all three of them. Nor are they separate. If a man's faith in his message is undermined, or if (believing in the message) he has ceased to believe in preaching as the best means of its proclamation in the modern age, how will he guard his devotions and "hang on a crucified God" to put him in mind of his promise: "Ye shall receive *power* when the Holy Ghost is come upon you"? [1] If, deeply believing his message, he nonetheless scamps his devotions on the assumption that he can do the work alone, or despises the technique of his calling in the mistaken idea that there is nothing about preaching that can be taught, what hope is there that the people in their turn will hang upon his words and go away knowing that God has spoken to their souls?

The quest for power in preaching involves research, therefore, in the sheer craft of homiletics; it involves learning how to become and how to remain a channel of the Holy Spirit; it involves ceaseless vigilance to keep intact within the soul the citadel of faith both in the gospel itself and in preaching as God's supreme method in its proclamation.

It is with that third task that I would deal here. I would ask any preacher eager to do his work better, or wondering at his ineffectiveness in the pulpit (and humble enough not to blame it on the people), or secretly wishful (as some are) to be out of the pulpit altogether, to put this question to his own mind: "Do I believe in preaching?"

[1] All power in preaching comes ultimately from the Holy Spirit. See "The Plus of the Spirit" (ch. ii in my *The Approach to Preaching*).

Having put the question, let us treat it with seriousness. The disposition of some will be to brush it impatiently aside by saying: "Of course I believe in it. Would I be doing it if I didn't?" But that could be a shallow answer; many people go on doing things in which they do not deeply believe. Economics are involved with some of them. It is not easy to change one's career in middle life. And if no economics are involved —as with a lay preacher, for instance—it is often easier to go on doing in some fashion or other what you have been doing and are expected to do than to make a rupture with your past life and disappoint the hopes of old friends.

Moreover, faith is not a matter of fact merely but a matter of degree. It is not enough to say—as the father of the epileptic boy realized—"I believe." The next question you must face is this: "How deep is my belief?" The fact is that one can sincerely believe with a couple of layers of the mind and doubt with all the rest. What Christian has not had the experience of praying for something "in faith" and of then being astonished when it happened? The astonishment measures the unbelief. It is clear already that no simple Yes answers the question I am posing. You believe in preaching? How much do you believe in it?

Many a young man has heard the call to preach and given himself to it with a fine zeal. He may, indeed, commit himself to it with lifelong vows and start with splendid enthusiasm.

But life brings a strain upon him. He can be tested

15

in all kinds of ways. His faith in God's love may be strained when he sees his own baby die in convulsions or one of his children turns out to be a mongol. His faith in the usefulness of preaching may be tested when all the outpourings of his soul beget no obvious response among his people and they remain petty-minded and given to bickering. Something happens inside him. Honestly, he is not sure himself what it is. He may even deny that anything is different. But other people notice it. He does not seem the same man who set out ten years ago. The duties are done, but there is no glow about them. The service has been conducted and the sermon preached. No charge lies against him. But no nimbus rests on him either. He would hotly—and justly —rebut any suggestion that he was an unbeliever, but what has happened? Why does he not run to the pulpit with eagerness, as a man would run who was utterly sure that he had an urgent message from God? What is this secret longing in his soul for some post that would make the pulpit less demanding, something administrative or of more obvious social use? Is it the gospel he is less sure of, or is it preaching as the means of proclaiming the gospel? It could be either or both. Only one thing is certain in all this fog of uncertainty: there is no power in his pulpit. No pulpit has power if it lacks deep faith in the message itself and in preaching as God's supreme method in making his message known.

Men who retain faith in the message, though little in preaching, tend to put the major stress of their work on other aspects of the Church's activity and sometimes openly disparage the service of the pulpit. Preaching, they argue, does little or nothing. The few people who come to worship have heard it all already. Pastoral work is infinitely more important, they say, or clubs, or drama. Whether the preaching is good or bad, the people have forgotten it by the time they get home.

Oh yes, the services must still be held. It is expected. But nothing else appears to be expected—no voice from Sinai, no tryst with heaven. Power has gone out of preaching when those whose task it is to preach have come to doubt the worth of it themselves.

So we face the question "Do I believe in preaching?" already aware of its complexity. We recognize some ambiguity in the question itself; it could mean, "Do I believe in the message?" or "Do I believe in preaching as the means of making it known?"

We recognize the depth as well as the ambiguity of the question. We may believe in one and not the other. Or we may half-believe in either or both. The termites of unbelief may be working at our faith in the gospel or at our faith in preaching. A bit of faith in both may survive in a man who goes on with a certain dutifulness in his work—yet only a bit. Haunted by the memory of the man who put his hand to the plow and looked back, he keeps in the furrow though he plows neither deep nor straight.

How can one's faith in preaching be recovered—and made deeper than it ever was? One cannot say, "Go to. I will believe in preaching." The recovery of faith is not the fruit of a simple act of will like that. Nor can it be achieved by a "pep talk" or a chapter in a book. The fruitlessness and disappointment of the years are not so easily dispelled.

But if a man was deeply serious about this and eager to give his utmost to the highest in whatever years remained, here are five things I would advise:

I

Nourish your faith in the gospel itself

Faith is a gift in its origin, but it becomes a virtue by the care we take of it. To regard our quality of faith at any time as fortuitous and varying in strength with the "vagaries" of the divine will is blasphemous. How much and how firmly we believe depends in large measure upon ourselves. What can convince a man of the power of prayer so much as hours spent in it? What makes a man one half so sure that Christ breaks the power of canceled sin as the experience in his own heart?

Doubts assail every intelligent mind. If the doubt is allowed to pass unchallenged into the subconsciousness; if, having gone there, it is allowed to remain undisturbed; if in his clearest, deepest thinking and his hardest, costliest praying a man does not take that doubt out and wrestle with it and hew it to pieces before the Lord— that harbored doubt will take terrible toll. This is the food of those termites of unbelief. This is how the faltering note creeps into the preacher's voice. This is how he comes to live in a twilight of half faith and half doubt.

Nothing can excuse the preacher from the toil of secret thought and prayer. Regret it as he may, his people live in part upon *his* faith. Struggling for the bread of this life, they have so little time to find the bread of any other. It is part of our priestly office as preachers to prepare it for them. We fail them at the very point of their expectations if we fail to feed their souls, if they go away unnourished, if "the hungry sheep look up and are not fed."

A preacher should guard the central citadel of his own faith as a sentry guards a beleaguered city. We live in a world of unbelief. Nature herself wears at times a God-denying look. The very issue of the battle turns upon faith. "This is the victory that hath overcome the world, even our faith."

One can keep one's job as a preacher with enough faith to go through the motions. But to feed the people —for that one must have deep faith, faith which amounts to certainty and which rules in all the inward parts.

II

Recognize that the gospel, being a revelation, can be known only as it is proclaimed

The Christian religion is not a philosophy. It can be philosophically stated, it can use philosophy, but it can never be equated with it.

Philosophy can be worked out of a man's mind. Picture Rodin's "The Thinker"; see the bent head resting on the back of the right hand and the left forearm droop-

19

ing over both knees. He is alone and he is naked; all his life reposes in his brain; nobody tells him anything; nobody needs to; he is thinking—thinking. That would serve as a picture of philosophy.

But the Christian religion is not philosophy. No man could work it out of himself. No one could know unless he was told.

Told what? That God is there and God is love; that God is like Jesus merciful and tender; that God came to earth as a man, lived the perfect life, died on the cross, rose from the dead, and will live in us forevermore.

No one could know unless he was told. "How then shall they call on him in whom they have not believed? and how shall they believe in him whom they have not heard? and how shall they hear without a preacher?" (Rom. 10:14.)

It may be said reverently—and explained more deeply in a moment—that not even the Almighty God could maintain his Church on our earthly plane without the preacher.

No wonder then that God made his only Son a preacher, that the first thing we are told of Jesus actually doing in the oldest of our Gospels is "Jesus came into Galilee preaching" (Mark 1:14), that when Jesus commissioned the Twelve he sent them forth first to preach and then to heal (Matt. 10:7-8). The Church has had the modern youth club for over thirty years, the motion picture and Girl Scouts for over forty, Sunday schools for a little more than 170, and preachers for nearly two thousand.

How shall they hear without a preacher? How, indeed? Being a religion of revelation, Christianity can be known only as it is proclaimed. On his way to preach the gospel the most modest man may whisper to himself: "Nothing more important will happen in this town this week than the work I am doing now."

III

Grasp the fact that the heart of the gospel
is a meeting of God and man, and preaching
provides the best medium for that meeting

Many people—many preachers even—find this hard to believe. They believe the gospel, and they believe that it must be proclaimed. What they cannot believe is that there is anything sacrosanct in preaching as the method of proclamation. The apostle Paul, of course, said that "it was God's good pleasure through the foolishness of preaching to save them that believe" (I Cor. 1:21), but printing was not invented then, nor the motion picture, nor radio, nor television—and even the drama was in a primitive form. They have come to believe that there are better ways of proclaiming the gospel than by preaching—the film, for instance, or religious drama; a pageant could do it or a book.

And who can deny some force in this? A thousand will look at television for every ten who go to church. People love a "show," and if the show can be sanctified

21

and do the work, need we worry by what road the wanderers travel so long as they travel home?

Now all this is plausible, but it is not convincing to those who know the nature of the gospel. That God uses these ancillary methods, we do not deny, but we maintain that preaching is *primary in the purpose of God.* "It was God's good pleasure *through the foolishness of preaching* . . . ." It is God's good pleasure still.

It does not turn on what people like but on what he likes. It is a question not of our particular gifts but of the divine intention. As H. H. Farmer says: "The activity of preaching is not merely a means for conveying the content of the Christian faith, but is in a real sense *bound up with that content itself.*" [2] "The necessity of preaching resides in the fact that when God saves a man through Christ he insists on a living, personal encounter with him here and now in the sphere of present personal relationships." [3]

Now that is the kernel of all this. We may be glad that the truth so long obscured is coming back to recognition again and that the "rediscovery of the significance of preaching" is regarded as the "most central and distinctive trend in contemporary Christian theology." [4] Though we find it difficult to explain at any time how God becomes real to a man, arrests him and changes his life, we know that there is a *meeting*—the I-Thou relationship of Buber's well-known phrase.

[2] *The Servant of the Word,* p. 14.
[3] *Ibid.,* p. 27.
[4] *Ibid.,* p. 9.

No medium offers God the conditions he is seeking so much as preaching—a man speaking to men, saturated with his prayer-drenched message, unimpeded by paper, looking the people in the face and saying, "You —you." The arbiters of refinement may think this "too beastly personal" and prefer the preacher who hides himself in that silly impersonal "One." But God is seeking to break through and challenge that wayward soul, or speak peace to that broken and contrite heart, or give clear guidance to that befogged mind, and this is the way he normally chooses to do it.

We may perhaps see here part of the deep underlying truth that God never enters into *exclusive* relationships with a soul, so that our ties with him always involve our ties with one another. Be that as it may. This at least we begin to glimpse—*why* preaching has primacy. The celluloid filmstrip has its place no doubt, and the television screen, and the printed page; but it is through a man preaching that God gets nearest to men. And those who still dislike the idea must remember again that it is not *their* likes which matter—but his.

IV

*Remember all that God has done
through preaching in the past*

He has changed lives this way—a multitude of them, a multitude which none can number. If that is less obvious today in Britain, it only illustrates again that religion is in partial eclipse. Throughout the centuries God has honored his own primary medium and broken

23

through the preacher to a "meeting" with millions of souls. Eternal consequences hang upon preaching.

He has changed towns this way—Boston and Kidderminster leap to one's mind. The whole life of Boston was affected by the ministry of Phillips Brooks. Under the preaching of Richard Baxter, Kidderminster simply ceased to be the same town. It was transformed from a coarse and brutal assembly of people to a town in which almost every home observed family prayers and an irreligious man was a rarity.

He has changed countries this way. England was not the same country at the end of the eighteenth century as it was at the beginning. Historians are emphatic on the point. They may like or dislike John Wesley and George Whitefield, but they cannot deny the influence of their preaching; England was changed. From the watershed of the evangelical revival streams of social reform have been flowing ever since.

He has changed the world this way. That the world is not completely changed to the will of God, we are all smartingly aware, but it is doubtful if our race could have survived until now but for the preaching of the apostles and their successors. Preaching shaped all the early centuries of the Christian Era; if the white race, foremost in the field of scientific discovery, had known nothing of the restraints of Christ, it is possible that the human race would have vanished from the earth. It has shaped the modern centuries too. The Reformation bore upon the people largely through preaching; Luther, Calvin, and Knox have left a legacy of writing,

but it was through their preaching that they shaped
their age.

V

Conserve what preaching has done in your own life

Few things buttress one's faith in preaching so much
as the proof of its power in one's own life. A scrap of
personal experience may only illustrate our human
vanity, but it is more weighty with us than much history.

If a man first came face to face with God under
preaching, he will not forget it. Spurgeon never forgot.
Growing up in a minister's home, he was wrapped
around with Godly influences from his earliest years,
but it was through the words of a simple preacher in a
Methodist chapel in Colchester that God really con-
fronted him with the I-and-Thou relationship. Many
efforts have been made to analyze Spurgeon's singular
pulpit power; some speak of his fine natural voice and
others of his limpid Saxon style, but deeper than these
undoubted qualities was this: that Spurgeon never went
to his pulpit without remembering that it was under
preaching that all things became new for him, and the
hope was ever in his heart as he opened the Holy Book
and gave out his text that so it would be for some sick
soul within range of his voice that day. Expectation
filled him, and he took aim.

If it was not under preaching that a man himself met
God, he will nonetheless treasure the recollection of
any who met God under his own preaching. This is not

vanity. The strengthening and deepening and extending of a preacher's own faith in preaching is so important that it is his duty humbly to remember before God the use which God has made of his words. It may not often (to his knowledge) have led to someone's conversion. But it may have led a vast deepening of faith, or its salvaging in sorrow, or its strengthening in doubt. A man who is on his face before God in secret prayer is not damaged by a word of gratitude. Indeed, people in Britain (the situation is different in America) might be encouraged to say (or write) a little more frequently than they do the thanks they must often feel to a faithful preacher whom God has used to bless their souls. One has heard of devoted men who go for months and years without the tonic of knowing that people have been helped. Well—they will still go on with their work. They have "meat to eat that [the world] knows not of." But how ungrateful it seems and how costly the omission might prove. An awful impoverishment falls upon the whole Church if the preachers themselves lose faith in preaching.

I recall a time in my life when I was on the edge of breakdown. Bereavement, serious sickness in the home, and gross overwork had brought me to a state of physical, mental, and spiritual prostration. I took a glance into that awful abyss of nervous illness the full horror of which is known only by those who have fallen in.

I was asked to attend a meeting in the center of the town. All the churches had been urged to support it, but I felt no enthusiasm. I was low-spirited, and the well-known preacher was not a man from whom I expected help.

I went, and that meeting has blessed me through more than twenty years. I knew from the second sentence that God was speaking through him to me. I sat in a back seat and could have wept. When it was over, I remained in a dazed wonder marveling that other people seemed not to have been ravished by it also, and when I went home, I was consoled in my sorrow, restored in my faith, and inwardly healed.

I often go to speak at meetings with that memory in mind. I find myself praying that somebody's awful extremity may be met. I whisper to God out of my unworthiness: "Do it again, Father!"

2

KEEP TO CENTRALITIES

Sermons can be classified in three major ways: (*a*) by their subject matter, (*b*) by their central structure, (*c*) by the psychological method employed in their presentation.[1]

Classification according to subject matter varies with different authors on homiletics, but the division which I have found serviceable and have used elsewhere is six-fold:

1. Bible Interpretation
2. Ethical and Devotional
3. Doctrinal
4. Philosophic and Apologetic
5. Social
6. Evangelistic

No superiority is claimed for this classification over others, and it is freely admitted by all teachers of preach-

[1] See *The Craft of Sermon Construction*, chs. ii, iii, iv.

ing that the edges of these classifications are not sharp; a sermon may possibly come under two or three designations.

Nonetheless, a clear example of one is easily recognizable and is not to be confused with a clear example of another, and it is a help in handling the wide variety of forms which the sermon takes to have legitimate types of preaching clearly in mind.

It does something else also. Many things pass as sermons which would not come under any of these categories. The preacher has been talking for twenty minutes, but it was not biblical interpretation or doctrinal teaching; it was not—except in the most anemic way—ethical or devotional material; certainly it was not Christian philosophy or a fighting defense of the faith; and just as certainly it did not expound the social nature of the gospel or call the sinner home. Was it, in fact, in any robust sense Christian teaching at all? A Christian man talking in a pulpit with an open Bible in front of him is not necessarily preaching the eternal gospel.

If it is argued—as it may legitimately be argued—that sometimes the preacher is required to deal in the pulpit with things other than the offer of God in Christ, it should always be possible for him to prove the close relation of his theme to the gospel once delivered to the saints, and certainly to show that it can be classified in the categories I have distinguished above. Only so can we face one of the chief dangers of modern preaching—its perilous tendency to get away from the centralities of the faith.

I

*All the evidence goes to show that a great deal
of Protestant preaching for a generation past
has been on marginal things*

This dangerous preoccupation with nonessentials has
been noticed by the observant both in Britain and in
America. When Bishop Kulandran looked at America
through oriental eyes and studied in particular the
message of the American pulpit, nothing struck him
more than its astonishing silence on deep theological
issues. Social optimism he found and an "appeal to
goodness," but the "great affirmations about ultimate
matters" were never sounded in his ears, and he could
not make up his mind whether the silence was to be explained on the ground that those great affirmations were
not deemed to be true or were thought unimportant.[2]
The bishop must have been wrong about *some* of the
pulpits in America. Was he wrong about the American
pulpit taken as a whole?

What of the Protestant pulpit in Britain? Can anyone
familiar with the facts feel comfortably assured that
Bishop Kulandran might not have brought a similar
condemnation against British preaching? And if he did,
he would be wrong again about *some* pulpits and right
about so many more. The anonymous but able layman
who discussed in *The Times Literary Supplement* some
years ago the problem of the empty pews had this

[2] Sabapathy Kulandran, *The Message and the Silence of the American Pulpit.*

30

criticism to offer on British preaching: "It was too scanty and did not strike deep enough." He asked for more of the "innermost truths of Christianity." [3]

In 1949 a group of educationalists after a careful survey of preaching in their various denominations addressed a plea to church leaders for more systematic teaching from the pulpits. They asked for continual instruction in doctrine and Christian ethics, and regretted that the older exegetical and didactic sermon had been largely replaced by a topical address. [4]

If the sermon titles which are printed on Saturday evenings in some newspapers are anything to go by, many preachers are still toying with trifles. Nor is it a fault only of the less able men. One sometimes hears a man with a good deal of homiletical skill weaving something out of nothing in the pulpit and leaving the heart-hungry listener wishing that half that cleverness had been spent on the marrow of the gospel and had dealt in a serious way with the things by which men live.

It is not without interest to inquire how preachers got into this way of misusing their time and attempting the impossible task of making a staple diet out of sugary trifles.

1. To begin with, it is easier. Teaching-preaching is one of the hardest parts of the homiletical craft.

[3] October, 1944. Charles Morgan was the author. See his *Reflections in a Mirror* (Second Series).

[4] "Topical preaching" is variously defined. See *The Craft of Sermon Construction*, pp. 56 ff.

2. It was thought to be more interesting. In the hands of the inexpert, doctrinal preaching was heavy and uninviting and (grotesque misunderstanding!) seemed unrelated to daily life; and by contrast the people were grateful to a preacher who fixed on some incident of current life already in their minds and commented on that. The gratitude of the people for their deliverance from doctrine not well taught spread the idea that theological preaching was unpopular and out of date. Men who dreaded more than anything else to be out of date slipped into the fashion and slipped the more easily because it was the easier thing to do. They even smiled superciliously on those who kept to the harder, older way. Archbishop Leighton had to protest in his day: "Surely, when all of you are preaching up the times, you may allow one poor brother to preach up Christ and eternity."

3. It was only a development of this state of mind when men became more eager to say something *new* than to say something *true*. They were ensnared by novelty. Instead of bending their strength to make the familiar fresh and to show its eternal significance, they fretted around to find something nobody had said before. They looked for "odd" texts which on their announcement might make the congregation wonder: "Whatever will he get out of *that?*"

So they reversed the Bible judgments on its own characters. Judas Iscariot was white-washed, and Moses was blackened. Peter did not really deny his Lord; he was a spy, and lying is part of a spy's technique. Martha had the "better part," though Jesus said that it belonged to Mary.

Dubious identifications were sought. Was John Mark the son of the "goodman of the house" in Mark 14:14? Was the rich young ruler Lazarus, or the companion of Cleopas on the Emmaus road his wife? Speculations were raised concerning unimportant people who flit across the Bible record. Who was the young man who followed Jesus out of Gethsemane and then fled naked from the scene (Mark 14:51-52)?—as if it mattered either way. And while all this was going on, the basic truths were left aside as being too obvious to mention, or somewhat dubious, or quite unimportant. Like Bishop Kulandran, the hearer was often unsure which.

4. Nor do the explanations of this drift from centralities end even there. Some men, properly impressed with the importance of illustrations in sermons, came to exaggerate the truth that they had seen. "We live in a picture age," they said. "Pictures mean everything. Televison, the motion picture, illustrated magazines— all point the same way. Pictures are our need." Instead of keeping the illustrations subservient to the thought and calling for pictures only when the framework of a well-wrought sermon was in shape, they strung together a few illustrations which pleased them and let the illustrations make the sermon. "Anyhow," they said, "it is only the illustrations which people remember."

They did not see that it does not matter a fig if people remember an illustration unless they remember also what important thing it is illustrating, and if there is no important thing to illustrate, it is all a waste of time. I think it was W. M. Macgregor who was taken to worship once by a friend who was eager that Macgregor should hear a new preacher he had found. The sermon was a string of loosely related pictures illustrating nothing important, and the friend regretted the persuasion he had used. They walked home in silence. Finally—and in a desperate effort to find something good to say—he said to Macgregor: "Well, it was a nice children's address he gave." *"Two* children's addresses," said Macgregor.

Whatever the reasons, the fact, I think, is plain enough. For a generation past the Protestant pulpit in Britain and America has dealt too much with marginal things. Somebody said once of Matthew Arnold that he was a melancholy preacher who had mislaid his gospel. How far that was a fair comment on Matthew Arnold, we may leave aside, but the latter part is *not* an unfair comment on many modern preachers. Certainly they have mislaid *their* gospel. A severer censure it would be hard to frame, and all of us who stand in pulpits may well search our own hearts and say, as the apostles said on that dark, betrayal night: "Is it I, Lord?"

II

All honest scrutiny of the deep need of men and women
stresses the supreme importance
of doctrinal preaching

1. It is a *message* we have to give.

Christianity is not vague sentiment. It is not in its

34

essence an amiable feeling. It is not (in the language of the little boy) "being kind to grandmother and the cat." It has a hard, dogmatic core. It centers in a living Person, but it builds on certain historical facts concerning that Person, and it is tied to a number of immense affirmations regarding God, man, and the universe.

It is not Christianity when these are cut out. If the faith is watered down to a mild good will, it has ceased to be the faith once delivered to the saints.

It has been the disposition of some people to dismiss the dogmatic heart of Christianity as unimportant, as theorizing, and as speculative. If one was busy with practical service, it was suggested, the theory could be largely left aside. It would be bold perhaps to *deny* it, and after all there might be something in it; but the important thing was to do the "good works," and the good works, it seemed, could be produced whether the dogma was received or not.

The consequences of this attitude—held, for instance, by some missionaries to China—have had repercussions that may last for centuries. D. W. Brogan says:

Many missionaries only twenty years ago were content to bring literacy and medicine and modern science to the heathen, no longer thought of as sitting in theological darkness, though, in secular ways, in great need of light. And this attitude, it should be remembered, had an important political effect. For the "modern" missionaries were less alarmed by the doctrines of the Chinese Communists than their more orthodox brethren. They did not take formal doctrine seriously themselves; why should they expect Mao to do so? [5]

"They did not take formal doctrine seriously themselves"—that is the gravamen of the charge. But the Communists did—and do—believe in their doctrine. It is from *doctrine*, held passionately and without deviation, that practical consequences flow. What satanic power blinds amiable people to this plain truth and leads millions to say: "How can it matter *what* I believe if I'm kind?" Kindness itself perishes when the root from which is springs is dead. Christian doctrines are the roots from which all the fine fruits of the gospel rise. A first duty of the Christian preacher, therefore, is to teach doctrine.

2. But doctrine, as we have seen, is neglected.

One explanation sometimes offered for the neglect of doctrine is that it is all perfectly understood already and that to deal with it is to labor the obvious.

Nothing is more remote from the fact. Doctrine is not understood. People do not know the faith. How little Christianity is known in "Christian" Britain was revealed with painful frankness in a speech at Portsmouth by Admiral Sir Geoffrey Layton.[6] He said that he had set a simple examination in religious knowledge to the young men joining the Navy under his command. They represented a cross section of the population though, he thought, above the average in general intelligence.

[5] *Manchester Guardian,* February 28, 1953.
[6] January, 1947.

Only 23 per cent could repeat the Lord's Prayer accurately; 28 per cent knew it in part; 49 per cent knew no more than the opening words.

Although 72 per cent knew who Jesus Christ was, only 39 per cent knew where he was born. What happened on Good Friday was known to 62 per cent, but only 45 per cent knew about Easter, and only one man in forty could explain Whitsuntide. Sir Geoffrey discovered abysmal ignorance on other aspects of the faith as well. It passes comprehension how anyone can believe that Christian teaching is understood in Britain today.

It will be said, of course, that most of these young men were outside the Church and that the preacher has to concern himself with those who are inside. Though people outside may know next to nothing of doctrine, it is argued that the people inside know it quite well and do not need constant iteration.

But again, this is not true. It is the unusual Protestant church in which doctrine is carefully and systematically taught. If preachers are proceeding on the assumption that it is all understood, the assumption is a false one. If preachers do suppose that some complete—if simple —outline of theology already lies in the minds of their hearers to which they are under obligation to make only occasional and passing reference, it is a dangerous supposition and illustrates again what Richard Gehman called the "vague specific."

He illustrates the vague specific in a domestic setting by a conversation between his wife and the maid.

"Here," said the mistress of the house, "you can put these out there somewhere."

"With the others?" asked the maid.

"No," said the mistress decisively; "put them with those things behind the others."

"Conversation can go on like that," says Gehman, "for ten minutes." He calls it the "vague specific."

But the vague specific is worse in a dogmatic setting than in a domestic one. Sermons without teaching in them run their course with vague references to some body of belief which we all know (or do we?), sustained by sanctions we all accept (or don't we?), reared on a rock which cannot be moved (or can it?). The tragedy is that, little as the preacher may realize it, the vague specific in this context is not specific at all.

In the end the faith for which the martyrs died vaporizes into mild sentiment, and when you put your hand out to grasp it, there is nothing there.

3. Exhortation is not enough.

Faced with the fact that the faith is not being seriously taught from Protestant pulpits, an intelligent teacher in another segment of knowledge, or a propagandist of an alien faith, might well ask in bewilderment: "Then how do they fill the time? To what use is the sermon being put?" The answer is not simple.

In some communions the sermon time is whittled down to ten minutes, and the people are taught that even those ten minutes are not important. A false distinction is drawn between worship and preaching, and instead of seeing both in a large way and as belonging

together, the effort is made to exalt worship by be-
littling the sermon. After all, the sermon is only a man
talking; it cannot compare in importance with the
prayer and the praise.

There is no picture here of the preacher as a herald
from God, no conception of a man who has wrestled long
in prayer for his message, no deep digging in the Book
of books. Just a man talking! And—in the passing of
time—the quality of the preaching falls inevitably to
this low conception of it, and it becomes what its tra-
ducers described. Just a man talking! The hungry sheep
look up and are not fed.

Or—in those communions where the sermon still creates
a sense of expectation—a man may take his half an hour
for the sermon but specialize in topical events. He may
seize on some national or international piece of news
and retail it in a moral manner. No doctrine is involved
and no clear gospel either.

Or he may declaim against sin in general or warmly
appeal to people to respond to the "highest," and the
sermon becomes all exhortation. If it is done earnestly,
it can beguile the mind of the hearers for twenty minutes, until the thoughtful listener challenges the vague
specific and inquires of himself precisely what he was
being exhorted to (or from!), and on what clear
grounds, and by what plain authority.

Then a haze of uncertainty hangs over it all—inevitable in any ministry which has no clear and sustained
teaching at its heart. Exhortation has its proper place

when the teaching has been given, but as a substitute for it, it is ludicrous. The foam on the ginger ale is pleasant to look upon, and it shows a certain liveliness in the drink, but it is quite unacceptable in place of the drink itself.

4. Power is generated in part by great belief.[7]

How power gets into preaching is not to be explained by *one* thing. Several elements combine to impart that mystic plus to preaching, but great belief is one of them.

Let a man be laid hold of by certain truths, let him see them as facts and not only as feelings, let him see them lying at the heart of reality and with immense significance, not only to himself but to the whole human race, and they will give an urge and warmth and conviction to his proclamation which is quite transforming. It can make the stammerer fluent—and sometimes make the overfluent stammer. Indeed, it makes much talk of diction seem pedantic. It puts deep notes into preaching which otherwise are never there. It can haunt the hearers afterward and challenge all their unbelief. Though they reject it at the last, they cannot reject it easily; it demands examination. One thing such preaching cannot do: it cannot just "wash over" people, leaving them unmoved by the experience. Those who would cling to earthly comforts must avoid it. Just to "come under it" is dangerous indeed.

No man, of course, can say to himself: "If great belief is necessary for great preaching, I will have great

[7] Cf. pp. 13-27 above.

belief." Great belief comes to a man by the power of the Holy Spirit and with the high authority of truth, and not as an aid in homiletics. But if it does not come, no aids of homiletics can take its place. The most they can do is to cover the absence in the preacher of deep belief in clearly grasped truth, and they have no hope of succeeding in that for very long. Preacher and people alike are aware of something missing. At the last that minister becomes as sounding brass or a tinkling cymbal.

Here, then, are plain questions every preacher of the gospel must pose to his own mind: "Do I hold the faith and have I taught it—or am I guilty of dealing mainly with marginal things? When did I last preach a series of sermons on the Creed, or expound the deity of Christ, or explain our redemption, the personality of the Holy Spirit, the doctrine of man, or the nature of the Church?"

Let it be conceded (as, indeed, we have conceded already) that there are occasions when teaching the central truths of the Christian faith does not appear to be the immediate business of the preacher. Temperance Sundays and harvest festivals are important in their way, and yet—from the viewpoint of doctrinal preaching—a little off center. But surely only a little! Both are meaningless if certain cardinal doctrines are false. Both can be handled with the faith on which they are dependent clearly in view. A ministry given chiefly to clear and appealing teaching of the creeds can sustain days of dealing with the inferences. Indeed, it demands them.

41

But the main staple of preaching *cannot* be the frills of things. Teaching the faith is of supreme importance.

III

Doctrinal preaching is not easy preaching,
but the people want it

All serious preachers know that different kinds of sermons vary in difficulty. Bible biography is not hard. Guided by the concordance, one heaps the facts together, broods over them, makes an interpretation, and the sermon is soon in shape. Sermons we have classified as devotional are not normally hard to make—so far as the sermon craft is concerned. The disciplined life of prayer which lies behind them and the insights they include may have been hard to win in the secrecy of one's own life with God, but when the hour comes for speaking of them, the homiletics are not difficult. The matter takes its mold without heavy labor, and the word is said.

But doctrinal preaching *is* hard—if it is to be gripping as well. A cold repetition of textbook theology could be knocked together, I suppose, without any "blood, toil, tears and sweat," but it would bore the people and empty the church. Making doctrine interesting is the skillful thing. The very *craft* of preaching is to take the theological facts—which may be truisms to some hearers and pious impossibilities to others—and make them shine with immense significance and become the glowing truths by which the people live.

What a task! Only a moron could think it simple; but

a serious servant of the Word would be challenged by the sheer difficulty of it and thrill at the thought that the people could be drawn to church—first, of course, to worship, but also out of sheer interest in the teaching itself.

But the people can be so drawn, because—contrary to the common idea—they secretly *want* this kind of preaching. Sad experience has made them dread too much theology in the pulpit, and it is wise not to talk of it as doctrinal or theological preaching, but in their heart of hearts they want to understand the faith. "Teaching-preaching" is a term they will not resent. A man facing the same congregation twice a Sunday could gladly give one sermon to this. Based squarely on the Bible and closely related to daily life, it is the sort of preaching to which the people will rise like hungry trout in the cool of evening; and when their faith is challenged by the men with whom they work, they will not take refuge in describing their feelings or pleading for a vague good will, but they will state what they believe and give a reason for the hope which is in them.

Militant unbelievers (like the Communists), holding with passionate intensity their own clear articles of unbelief, will not be withstood by some amiable appeal to goodness. They have their own ideas of what the term "goodness" can be made to mean, and they know the way to it. Their sacrificial earnestness is the aura of their great belief, and their constant preaching of doctrine is proof in itself that plain people will take doctrine if it can be made plain enough.

Here, then, is the preacher's task: to preach about God, to show man his own real nature, to expose sin, to announce the way of salvation, to stagger people with the truth of the Incarnation, to hold up in a hundred ways the wonder of atonement, to tell of the work of the Holy Spirit, and to proclaim all the refinements of grace.

These are the foundation truths which sustain people in great trouble. When the doctor abandons hope, when a dear one is certified insane, when a child bent on wickedness breaks your heart, when some awful, natural disaster seems to deny the existence of a good God, when the coffin is standing beside the bed, graceful little essays about nothing in particular are no good, and the poor souls which have been fed upon them in place of robust preaching have nothing to rest on.

When all is said and done, the questions which every thinking being wants answered amid the chances and changes of this mortal life are very few. Is God there? Does God care? Is there a meaning in life? Does life go on? What is God's purpose with me? If there is a heaven, how may I go there?

Only the preaching which offers a convincing answer to these questions is preaching directed to the people's need. Teaching-preaching does that. It speaks to people's need. It deals with centralities. And no sustained ministry is worthy which fails to do that.

3

WORK AT IT

It ought to go without saying that preparation for preaching involves the hardest work, but two reasons make it necessary to say it again and again.

Some preachers have persuaded themselves that the inspiration of the Holy Spirit makes all work unnecessary, and other people (who are not so crass as that) believe, none the less, that the divine nature of the task should convert it all into joy—they argue that there should be "no irk in the work" which is really done for God.

It will be of value if we look at each of those viewpoints in turn.

I

The Holy Spirit does not eliminate drudgery

1. No preaching is Christian preaching which is not undertaken in quiet reliance on the help of the Holy Spirit, but to infer from that unquestioned truth that a preacher is exempt from the toil of preparation is untrue

and, indeed, superstitious. Too many times it has been made a pious cloak for laziness and a shabby evasion of honest questioning of the truth of what was said. A preacher giving reasons for his message may be met by other reasons, and "good reasons must perforce give way to better." But a man refusing to discuss his message on the ground that it was all a private revelation of the Holy Spirit seeks to insulate himself from challenge and is on the way to that dangerous individualism which can be so great a snare in Protestant thought.

Any serious preacher with any length of experience could give striking illustrations of the help of the Holy Spirit in his pulpit preparation—and know, even as he gives them, that the half has not been told. Sometimes a whole sermon comes to him in one illuminating flash. Sometimes, having wrestled fruitlessly for days with some obscure passage of scripture or problem of providence, he finds that it splits wide open and knows that his own toiling effort was but a small part of the solution; the revelation had come from God. The thought and the text and the plan and the delivery are all shaped in a reverent mind by the Holy Ghost.

But to infer from this that a man is exempt from the labor of thought, and that he has only to open his mouth in a pulpit for the Holy Spirit to fill it, is to abuse a deep truth and to misdescribe the way God chooses to work with men.

The Rev. Greville P. Lewis was once conducting a conference of lay preachers. He had made a moving plea for the consecration of the whole mind to the service of the pulpit, but when the conference was thrown open for discussion, one preacher present rejected both the argument and the appeal. Study and thought and sermon outlines were all unnecessary, he said. At least they were unnecessary for *him*. He just prayed. Just that. Having prayed, he went to his appointment, opened the Bible for the text, and the Holy Spirit did the rest. He concluded by saying: "I have never failed for a message yet."

The uncomfortable silence which followed this flat contradiction of all the lecturer had said was finally broken by a man who appeared to be profane. "I never knew the Holy Spirit was so boring, repetitive, and unoriginal," he said. Urged to explain himself, he told the company that he worshiped at a church to which the previous speaker regularly came to preach. "I've heard him many, many times," he said. "The only thing that varies in what he says is the text. He certainly opens the Bible and takes a phrase at random, but whatever the text, after the first couple of sentences he always preaches the same uninspiring sermon. If he ever failed to appear, we could say it for him. You will notice how difficult I find it to accept his own explanation of his preaching. It would compel me to believe the impossible—that the third person of the blessed Trinity had nothing fresh and nothing moving and nothing mighty to say."

Into such an impasse do those people come who "toil not" and ascribe their vapid unrelated extemporizings to the direct and immediate inspiration of the Holy Ghost.

2. But not so easily rebutted are those who admit the need of disciplined thought in the preacher but do not care to describe it as "work" or "drudgery." The preacher ought always, they argue, to lose the duty in the joy. A sense of privilege and not of toil should mark all he does. A minister should run to his pulpit, they feel, murmuring within himself: "Fancy being paid to do this!"

It cannot be doubted that there is much of truth in this point of view. What is the difference between work and play at any time? It is a mental attitude. A professional golfer goes home at the end of the day weary with his work. A man who plays golf for fun—and not half so well as the professional—goes home after the same exertion thrilled with his recreation and only healthily tired. It is a superficial observation to say that the difference between work and play is that work is a thing that one has to do and play is a thing that one need not do. All regular work includes some elements of dull repetitiveness, but wise men learn by reason and will power to find interest in it, to enjoy the thrill of greater skill, and to get fun out of doing a job well.

A Christian does even more. Refusing to stay in any work that simply could not be done to the glory of God, he learns by more than reason and will power how to do his daily work to the sole praise of the Almighty, and all over the world the devout add luster to their labor by doing it for him.

If this is true of the Christian chimney sweep and housewife, how much more it ought to be of the Christian preacher. To urge a man called to preach to "work at it" should be quite unnecessary, some people argue, because the preacher's desires, and his sense of vocation, and his awareness of privilege, all point in the one constant way.

But none of this allows enough for the inertia of human nature. It is foolish to pretend that our sluggish comfort-loving dispositions do not often need to be dragooned into hard work. Anyone might get happiness out of doing a job well, and every Christian must learn in his own way to say:

> Accept my hallowed labour now,
> I do it unto Thee.

But hard work is collar work—especially at the start! Even a consecrated nature needs at times to be driven. Angels may fly on God's errands and know no emotion but joy, but our warped natures need discipline, and what preacher with any length of service but knows on occasion the need to push himself to his work.

Preachers do not clock in. Only God and their own conscience mark the misuse of precious hours, and the security of tenure which properly belongs to the ministerial office in most communions permits a man to get by on much less than a maximum.

That fact alone should move any preacher to welcome a call to still harder work. The man who was asked if he could play a violin and replied that he did not know because he had never tried has his parallels in the realms of preachers too. But if they mean to do it well, they will soon find out. It calls for hard work and demands its toll of hours. John Henry Jowett began life in a Yorkshire mill town where at five o'clock every morning the streets were noisy with the clogs of mill workers going to earn their daily bread. Jowett's lifelong habit of early rising was formed then. He could not bear the thought that those who labored for the bread which perished should be less eager than the one who toiled for the bread which perished not. Joseph Alleine was early to work and to prayer for the same reason. If he heard a tradesman plying his business before he was up, he was always distressed. "Does not my master deserve more than his?" he would ask. Bishop Fulton Sheen told Frederick Brown Harris that he gave on the average thirty hours of direct preparation for each of his twenty-two-minute radio talks. I have heard Leslie Weatherhead say that he has often written out a sermon five times. Whatever explanation people offer of the wide hearing given to these eminent men, they cannot say that their eminence was achieved without hard work.

A man must be left free to decide at what hours he can work best, and some will rise early and some will sit late, but a serious preacher will settle with himself that the stint of hours *must* be done and that the best work cannot be achieved without it.

I do not want any misunderstanding: it is *work*

for the pulpit that is in the forefront of my mind now. Many preachers work long hours and very hard (as we shall see in a moment) on work other than their work for the pulpit, and the work, no doubt, is accepted of God. But we are called to be *preachers*. To disparage or neglect our prime occupation for some other activity to which custom or inclination may prompt us is a widespread error of the modern ministry and explains in part the empty pews. No divorce can ever justly be made between prayer, preaching, and pastoral work. God has joined them together, and what God has joined together let no man put asunder.

Both prayer and pastoral work are indissolubly related to the pulpit. Faithful attention to them is necessary for the full discharge of our preaching function. But in addition to them preaching demands blocks of hours in every week for quarrying in the Book of God, wrestling to answer adequately in the pulpit the questions our people ask in their homes, and struggling to make clear, and plain, and appealing, the sometimes shadowed ways of God with men.

There is widespread criticism of preaching today— criticism not always heard by the preachers. People persuaded to go to church for the first time, or after the lapse of years, have sometimes written with bitter scorn of the sermons they have heard. Some of the criticism can be set resolutely aside. It was begotten of spleen and unbelief. But a great deal of it was honest and not unjust. Thoughtful men and women have felt that the ten minutes' "dribble" was insulting to their mental maturity and too jejune for words. They wonder how an intelligent man could inflict such sentiments upon a congregation. Perhaps it was of this that Dean Inge was thinking when he said that the work of the clergy—taken by and large—was the poorest professional work done in the country in his day.

We preachers may resent that. We have had more than our share of criticism, we feel. Yet the empty pews in thousands of churches are saying something pertinent, and it would be vain of us to clutch at every explanation except the one the people often give. It cannot be the *whole* explanation—radio and television explain something; so do good habits broken in the wars; so do rehousing schemes and the severance of old church connections. But the poverty of the preaching explains something also! Preaching consistently powerful and nourishing would call people back again to the house of God and might keep them there. And because that is a "consummation devoutly to be wished," no man need resent a call to work again and work harder at his pulpit preparation.

II

*"Busy . . . busy"—but with the priorities
all wrong*

How has it happened that men who once told the fathers of the Church that God had called them to preach, and who were subsequently ordained to that holy calling, often do not give to it with passing years the costly toil that it demands?

1. Some of them (as we saw in Chap. 1) have lost faith in preaching. They have never seen it *do* anything or never seen it do very much. That in itself may be a severe criticism of their preaching or a criticism of those who instructed them in the craft. It may also be (as we have seen) a comment on the dumbness of those who got help and never told the preacher so. But howsoever unbelief came, they have lost faith in preaching. They may never have openly admitted so much even to themselves, but that is the ground of their lost zeal. Preaching is just words—words—words! It does not do things.

Indeed, some preachers not only admit their unbelief in preaching; they rationalize it. The meetings where real business is done in religion, they argue, are not assemblies for worship but little meetings for fellowship and testimony. So they force into contrast things which were meant to be supplementary, and cannot see that powerful preaching can so challenge the sinner, and quicken the desire for more graces in the good, that the larger services can recruit the smaller meetings, and the smaller meetings complete the work that preaching began.

But in any case the explanation is clear: they have lost full faith in preaching.

2. It follows as a consequence that a hard-working minister can give what I judge to be a disproportionate amount of time to other occupations. The occupations vary in importance. He may become absorbed in psychology, or in religious drama, or in religious films. Clubs, operettas, or the finesse of administration may

53

obsess him. Ministers have won a wide reputation as conjurors, escapologists, and habitués of men's service clubs. Nor would I suggest, even by an innuendo, that there is no place for any of these things in the ministerial life, or that a man, giving his main strength to his main task, may not legitimately, and by the will of God, have an interest in a related occupation too.

But the peril of these ancillary callings is that they filch more and more time from the chief task and may become so large a part of a man's life that sermon preparation is scamped. A congregation can be consistently offered sermons prepared years ago for some other church, or given something thrown together hastily which might be expected to spread out thin for twelve or fifteen minutes.

Yet always there are some people present who sense the stale or shoddy workmanship—usually the people we should most like to grip and hold. Steadily they have drifted from the churches. Some fault attaches to them, no doubt, in that they are disobeying the apostolic injunction in not assembling themselves together and disregarding in addition the example of our Lord. But does not some blame attach to us preachers also who have not fed them on the pure wheat of the word?

3. Still other preachers have come to neglect their preparation for the pulpit on the ground that a simple, hastily prepared word has often appeared to help the people more than a thoroughly prepared message. More gratified comments have followed upon it, and these preachers have come to think that we overestimate

54

both the desire and capacity of our people. "Be simple," they say. "You can never be too simple. Our folk comment on our children's addresses with more appreciation than on our sermons, and there is a clue in that. In the things of religion they are not specialists. Treat them as babes."

A good deal of truth and falsehood is mingled in a statement like that. It often happens that the people most easily gratified are the people who most readily express themselves. What of the keener, more mature minds of the congregation? When do they get their turn?

The truth is that our people want the hardest questions answered, and they can take the thickest thinking so long as it is taken a bit at a time and put in the plainest terms. Putting it plainly (a matter with which we must concern ourselves in the next chapter) is part of the difficulty of the job. A man who throws half-digested theology at the people in technical terms and then complains that they simply cannot understand him is displaying nothing but his own stupidity and vanity. One of the tests of a serious craftsman is whether he can put a deep truth simply, light it up with vivid illustration, and tighten the grasp of his people on the very marrow of the faith. The simplicity that people justly ask for is the simplicity of profundity, not the simplicity of the kindergarten; the simplicity of the deepest, soundest scholarship, not the simplicity of infants in arms. It insults the maturity and life experience of our hearers, as well as expressing our own foolish pride, to suppose that if we take the trouble to make it plain, they are incapable of understanding the best that we can give. Life has been teaching them if books have not. Gone are the days when an educated pulpit addressed an uneducated pew. Talking down to people is vain as well as foolish and will leave us at the last with the kind of morons such preaching presupposes the people to be. And yet for preaching of the quality which is clearly called for, there is no substitute for consistently hard work.

III

How to think with God

Is it possible to say anything particularly useful of the kind of work that preaching demands?

Of the need for Bible study, the philosophy of religion, the interpretation of doctrine, and the multiform molds the sermon may legitimately take, I have written elsewhere[1] and I need not repeat myself now. But it may be of value if I write of that form of mental concentration which I call "prayer-thought," with which I am persuaded that all serious preachers are familiar, but which (with our incurable shyness in speaking of our own secret spiritual experiences) no writer of my acquaintance has discussed.[2] It is the supreme way, I believe, of preparing for the pulpit.

It is not prayer in the normal sense of the word—not

[1] *The Craft of Sermon Construction.*

[2] Some references are made in Frank Laubach's *Letters by a Modern Mystic.*

even prayer about preaching in general, or prayer about the service next to be led. (I shall have things to say about that kind of prayer in a final chapter.) It is not thought in the sense of wrestling on one's own with some problem of philosophy or casuistry. It is *prayer-thought*—a combination of the two and something different from either.

It is not meditation—or not meditation in the sense in which the great contemplatives normally employ the term. It is a conversation in the mind with God, and a conversation about that particular aspect of truth which the Holy Spirit has laid upon us as a message for the people.

Usually it comes to my aid in this way. I take the passage of scripture next to be expounded or the sermon which demands next to be prepared, and for a while I seem to have it largely to myself. I look at it in different lights, read the text in the original to see if anything of value lurks in the linguistics, turn it this way and that way in my thought. Much useful matter may be heaped together in that fashion. The bounds of the subject are well beaten. Possible ways of treatment come to view.

But all this may be—and often is—quite fruitless to yield a piercing insight to the heart of the subject or any inward certainty of the truth I must bring out.

Gradually my own efforts merge into prayer-thought. God comes into it. He deigns to hold a conversation in my soul upon the theme. Is it blasphemous to say so much? But then a preacher is a herald of the King, and if he goes only with his own word, he is something of a charlatan.

To those who have no experience of prayer-thought all this must sound slightly profane, but those who know it in experience will wonder that it is not better said.

When God comes and talks the matter over with his preacher, no words can describe the difference he makes. Quite often in my experience he just asks questions. And what questions!—questions that penetrate to the very heart of the matter and half carry their own answer in their utterance. Sometimes he takes over one's own tongue and just talks on the topic—but with what an infinity of difference from all the efforts on one's own. Sometimes he allows the preacher to ask *him* questions and often shows that his servant had the answer not fully grasped within his mind already.

So the colloquy goes on. Time and sense seem all no more. But this I am persuaded is how the sermons are made which do the real business of God. To every other kind of work and preparation this must be added. Only so does it become the message of the King—shaped, wrought, and fired by him. Only so can the preacher mount the pulpit steps inwardly sure that the word is not his but Another's. Only so can the gospel be uttered that the gates of hell do not prevail against it.

4

MAKE IT PLAIN

It is a common complaint among people who attend church that they do not understand what the preacher says. The complaint is still more common among people who, having lapsed from church attendance years ago or never having formed the habit, find themselves in a pew as virtual strangers. Even if they listen intently, they feel they have only a hazy idea of the meaning the preacher is seeking to convey, and if this disappointing experience is repeated several times, they may give up going to church altogether.

Some sympathy must be shown to the preacher in this dilemma. His is a hard task at any time. He has to speak of the things of heaven in the language and thought-forms of earth. The central doctrines of the Christian faith are not easily grasped even by a keen mind. Theology has its own technical language, and the favorite translation of the Bible is in semiarchaic speech. The preacher must take truths—some of which are deep and complex—and explain them in terms which are simple, dignified, and clear. It is no wonder that he often fails in the task and that few modest men in the "company of the preachers" would ever claim a full success.

There are senses in which preachers—in the French use of the word—are "vulgarizers." They have to take sublime truth and make it plain to common people. If it is said that Jesus Christ succeeded in doing that, part of the answer is that the teaching of our Lord had vast implications which the questing mind of man has been probing ever since and which must be faced even in the background of the parable of the prodigal son. Our Lord did not draw out those implications.

The simplest soul can ask the deepest questions. How can Jesus be both God and man? How does the Cross save? What is meant by the personality of the Holy Spirit? To essay the answer of these and similar questions for minds untutored in things theological is bold in the extreme. Yet that is the preacher's task. "The Lord gave the word: great was the company of those that published it." Great also was their task, and growing greater in some ways with passing time. How can the message be made plain? We have rejected as semicharlatan the practice of preaching mainly on things marginal, and see our task as teaching-preaching on matters undeniably deep. How is it to be done? What are the common dangers which preachers must avoid? How can we so mark the rocks and shoals of the course that we can sail securely in the deep water between?

I

There can be no clear speaking without clear thinking

No man can hope to be lucid in a pulpit (or anywhere else for that matter) who has not first *thought* himself clear. Nothing can take the place of disciplined thought. Only those who have gone over and over their theme in their minds and seen the path they intend to take from the announcement of the text to the concluding sentence can have any confidence in the clarity they will achieve. No man need (or ought!) to burden his mind with memorized words. If the thought is clear, adequate words can be commanded in the moment of utterance (and the ability to do this greatly increases with practice), but the thought *must* be clear and the path plainly in view.

The argument will begin there—and move to there—and there—and there, and the journey will finish at that point. I must be especially careful at the moments of transition, but I know what I'm going to say and I know the deposit of truth I will leave in the people's mind at the last. The congregation may reject the teaching, and possibly feel unattracted to me personally, but at least they will not be able to say that I was vague or that they did not know what I was "on about."

It is a great help to clarity to condense the message of your sermon to the length of a telegraph form and to chisel—as Jowett did before any writing began—one clear sentence which expresses the meaning the sermon is to convey. Plain words—as we must stress next—are

61

golden, but plain words ring true only when they are
minted in clear thought.

II

*There can be no clear speaking
if the words employed are not understood*

Preachers are prone to certain common errors of style.

1. Sometimes it is too self-consciously stylish.
John Wesley was a don at Oxford and as fond of a well-
turned sentence with a touch of grace as any of his
colleagues, and it is quite amazing to remember that
this was the man who made himself understood by the
uneducated masses all over England in the eighteenth
century. At the pithead, and the market cross, and on
Kennington Common, the poor people hung on his
words.

The reason is well known. When his heart had been
"strangely warmed," and he felt the call of God to
preach to the illiterate multitude, he sat down with his
sermon manuscript and a simple domestic servant, urg-
ing her to stop him at every word she did not understand. His manuscript became a maze of erasures and
interlinings, but he persisted until he had a speaking
style so plain and unpretentious that people with no
formal education whatever had no difficulty in following his thought. Some sacrifice, no doubt, was involved
in all this. Not without effort does a scholar strip himself in this way, throwing aside the graceful literary
allusion and the prose which borders on verse.

But Wesley was measuring himself to his task. He meant to be understood. All preachers should be understood. Preaching is not primarily a fine art. It is a medium for conveying urgent meaning. The man who uses it as a way of displaying his gifts has prostituted his high calling.

It is probable that all men of education who have had oratorical power over the people have undergone some similar discipline. Churchill did not say in June, 1940: "The position as regards the French military situation is extremely serious." He said: "The news from France is bad." The author of a life of Lord Salisbury writes less effectively when he tells us that "finance was the fly in life's fresh fragrant ointment." [1] He means that Lord Salisbury was short of money.

The preference for words of Saxon rather than of Latin origin can be made a fetish, but the rule is roughly right. The preference for monosyllables against polysyllables can also be exaggerated, but again the rule is roughly right. If you carry in mind a regard for the concrete as against the abstract word, for severe rather than adorned speech, and are on guard also against an overuse of adjectives, the style becomes more clear and taut. Many preachers muffle their meaning by overusing limiting phrases such as "generally speaking," "in a measure," "as it were." It takes all directness from their style. Russell Maltby told me once that he attended a committee on evangelism and heard one member pref-

[1] A. L. Kennedy, *Salisbury* (1830-1903), p. 30.

ace his remarks by saying: "Well, I suppose that we are all more or less and to some extent born again!"

In arguing against a manner of speaking too self-consciously stylish, no criticism of natural eloquence is intended. Let that come as it will. Rising spontaneously from the soul it will reach the heart of the people. But *labored* eloquence is not appealing; even those who like it are apt to sit and listen to the eloquence rather than to the meaning, and depart admiring the preacher rather than sorrowing for their sins.

2. Sometimes it is grossly flatulent.

It is only a step from speech self-consciously stylish to speech which is grossly flatulent. I was present in a meeting once at which a minister was asked to thank the ladies for making the tea. He solemnly expressed our deep gratitude to them for "socializing our intellectual intercourse." Howard Whitman in his book *A Reporter in Search of God* complained that something was not "amenable to verbalization." [2] He meant that it wouldn't go into words. Herbert Morrison, the labor leader, is reported to have said in a speech at Cardiff that we are not able to afford a "low-grade productivity in work." He meant that we should not be idle.

Preachers and politicians are both prone to flatulent speech, but perhaps the worst offenders in time past have been government officials. History does not record the name of the plumber who won a running battle over

[2] P. 114.

the jargon of bureaucracy, but his victory can be a warning to all who preach the Word.

He had written to a Washington department reporting that he had found hydrochloric acid good for cleaning out clogged drains, and he received this in reply: "The efficacy of hydrochloric acid is indisputable, but the corrosive residue is incompatible with metallic permanence."

The plumber sent a postcard saying: "Glad you agree with me."

Another letter came: "We cannot assume responsibility for the production of toxic and noxious residue with the use of hydrochloric acid." The plumber wrote again expressing his delight at having been of use.

Then he got this letter: "Don't use hydrochloric acid. It eats hell out of the pipes."

3. Sometimes it is too theological.

No one can justly complain of technical language in its proper place. It is verbal shorthand. Its proper place is in the conversation of experts. Specialists in all spheres use it—sailors, surgeons, chemists, biologists, philosophers, theologians. It saves time and makes for fine distinctions. Most games and hobbies have a minor technical language too. But the pulpit is not the place for the technical language of theology—or not much of it and only then when it has been explained.

The gospel was given to be preached. It was said of our Lord that the common people heard him gladly. It may justly be asked of anything which claims to be a part of the eternal gospel: Will it preach? If the teaching is so abstruse that it simply cannot be made plain to plain people, it may be doubted whether it belongs to the gospel once delivered to the saints.

In the company of his brother preachers a minister may indulge to the full his natural taste for theological discussion in theological terms, but in the pulpit he is dealing in the main with people who have no time, and perhaps no taste, for theological finesse, but who certainly need the bread by which men live. It is not to be inferred too readily that his hearers are his intellectual inferiors; he is a layman in spheres where they are specialists. But his task as a preacher is to say in clear nontechnical words what they need to know about God and his will, the way of salvation and the path to sanctity, the social consequences of the gospel and the rule of God in all life.

Some technical words cannot be avoided. He cannot preach the gospel with the word "grace," and it will be hard to avoid "incarnation" and "atonement," and so on. But technical words must be as few as possible and—without a trace of talking-down to the people—briefly explained. (Even a hint of intellectual superiority is offensive in the pulpit. The people can take the best that we can give them if we are at pains to make it plain.)

A writer tells of hearing a preacher in Chicago urge upon his congregation that "theistic metaphysics is pure theology." He faced an ordinary congregation and was probably incomprehensible to 99 per cent. It is a tragedy that professional work should be so poorly done.

It is more rather than less tragic if he deceived himself and some of his people with the idea that he was going over big.

I have already referred to the preaching style of John Wesley and marveled that an Oxford scholar could make himself so clearly understood in the highways and byways by the uneducated masses of the eighteenth century. It will not be without value to notice what he says on the subject.

In the introduction to a volume of his sermons, dated 1746, he says:

I design plain truth for plain people: therefore, of set purpose, I abstain from all nice and philosophical speculations; from all perplexed and intricate reasonings; and, as far as possible, from even the show of learning. . . . I labour to avoid all words which are not easy to be understood, all which are not used in common life; and, in particular, those kinds of technical terms that so frequently occur in bodies of divinity—those modes of speaking, which men of reading are intimately acquainted with, but which, to common people, are an unknown tongue.

This testimony is the more impressive when we remember the range and depth of Wesley's scholarship and that most of the sermons to which this was a preface carried considerable theological freight.

But he has words to say also concerning what I have called a manner of speech "too self-consciously stylish" and even that which I have disparaged as "flatulent." In his introduction to another volume of sermons (1788) he says:

> Is there need to apologize to sensible persons, for the plainness of my style? . . . I *could,* even now, write as floridly and rhetorically as even the admired Dr. ——; but I dare not. . . . What is the praise of man to *me,* that have one foot in the grave, and am stepping into the land from whence I shall not return? Therefore, I dare no more write in *fine style* than wear a fine coat. But were it otherwise, had I time to spare, I should still write just as I do. I should purposely decline, what many admire, a highly ornamented style. . . . Let who will admire the French frippery; I am still for plain, sound English.

When his advice was sought on the subject, he was compelled to answer in terms like these:

> Clearness in particular is necessary for you and me; because we are to instruct people of the lowest understanding. Therefore we, above all, if we think with the wise, yet must speak with the vulgar. We should constantly use the most common, little, easy words (so they are pure and proper) which our language affords. When I had been a member of the university about ten years, I wrote and talked much as you do now. But when I talked to plain people in the castle, or the town, I observed they gaped and stared. This quickly obliged me to alter my style, and adopt the language of those I spoke to. And yet there is a dignity in the simplicity, which is not disagreeable to those of the highest rank.

4. Sometimes it is too psychological.

A more serious offense than the overuse in the pulpit of theological language is the use of the technical language of psychology.

This has become very common in recent years. It was inevitable that the new psychology should command the close interest of preachers. The light cast upon hidden motives, new insights into the power of imagination and the shaping of ideals, shrewd guesses at the origin and fostering of fear, and so on, could not fail to fascinate the minds of those whose great concern was conduct. When you add to this the challenge which psychology has presented to all spirituality, and the disposition of its less able exponents to wipe out whole segments of human experience on the ground that "it all has a psychological explanation," it will be clear that it was the duty as it was the interest of preachers to become as expert in psychology as they could. Pastoral work and apologetics both demanded it.

What is not so clear is that preachers were under obligation to carry the ugly jargon of the psychologists into the pulpit. If there was little excuse for theological technical terms, there was still less for the technical terms of psychology. It was hard at times to resist the idea that the words were being used as an incantation, almost as a sly intimation that we have "caught up" with these psychological pundits as well.

So we had sermons on "schizophrenia" and the "subliminal." Congregations were taken through the tortuous paths of the subconscious in pursuit of "traumas" and "phobias." It was surprising after that to remember that Paul had discussed most of what was important on the subject without resort to this awkward language at all. "The good which I would I do not: but the evil which I would not, that I practise. . . . I see a different law in my members, warring against the law of my mind . . . . O wretched man that I am! who shall deliver me out of the body of this death?"

We may be thankful for every useful insight which the new psychology has given us without importing its jargon into our pulpits. The rustic who went to hear Dean Church wondered afterward if the preacher could be, after all, the learned man he had supposed. "I understood everything he said," he murmured. No doubt somebody told the simple man that that was a further proof of Dean Church's learning. Mature scholarship knows how to be plain.

5. Sometimes it is too Canaanitish.
I need not pause to explain what I mean by the "language of Canaan." The phrase has passed into current speech. I confess to a certain fondness of such language myself—when it is well used and in its proper place. It is made up of scraps of the King James Version of the Bible interlarded with bits of the hymnbook. There are few experiences more spiritually transporting than to be at devotions with those who have the gift of prayer and who speak with freedom in the language of Canaan.

> For heav'n comes down our souls to greet,
> And glory crowns the mercy seat.

The prayer meeting is the proper home of Canaanitish speech—and those fellowships where mature Christians foregather to enhearten one another on the heavenly way. No doubt some of this language penetrates the speech of all serious Christians. A minister of religion writing an article on a secular subject often betrays himself by traces of this style. The journalist calls it "parson's English."

But the pulpit is not its proper place. The hope of every preacher when he makes his way to worship is that some will come who have missed God's way for them, neglected church, been in the far country but are now turning their faces home.

The language of Canaan is strange to them. If they knew it once, they know it no more. It is imperative that the word of God reaches them clearly, and meaning can be muffled not only by "fine" speech, and "flatulent" speech, and technical speech, but by Canaanitish speech also. People strange to church have been urged to make their way there and to talk afterward of their experience, and not a few complain that the preaching was incomprehensible. William D. White asked twenty-five intelligent people in his congregation to list words and phrases they heard often in the pulpit and could not understand. Here are some of them: "lambent," "dayspring," "Logos," "husbandman," "washed in the blood," "blood of the Lamb," "throne

71

of mercy," "heir of salvation," "cherubim and sera-
phim," "alpha and omega," "things of the flesh," "balm
in Gilead," "bosom of Abraham," "in Christ"—the list
was almost endless. How futile it seems to spend so much
effort persuading people to come to church if when they
come they cannot understand what it is all about.

A mission report lies before me as I write. It is intended, I imagine, for any who may care to read. The
writer begins by protesting that "this is no fleshly boast-
ing." He speaks of "attempts of the enemy to mar the
work," but "we have confidence in him who is not un-
righteous, and honors those who set out in faith, perhaps
in much weakness and dependence upon him." He is
glad to report that there were many "numbered with
the saints in the assembly," who were "always keeping
in mind the overruling purpose, the salvation of precious souls." He is happy to assure the reader that the
"love of God was shed abroad in the hearts of be-
lievers."

Mr. S———, now with the Lord, was instrumental in
leading many to Christ. We meditate on our heavenly
Father's past mercies. Hitherto hath the Lord helped us
and, for the present, Jehovah Jireh. We earnestly look for
his coming again when he shall see the travail of his soul
and be satisfied and, whatever the future, here or here-
after, it is "Hallelujah." Should he in his longsuffering
still tarry, then we know that this also is well, and that he
will always honor our faith and dependence and obedience
to his Word.

What meaning all this would convey to the mind of a normal businessman invited to support the mission, I do not know. It might almost be written in a foreign tongue. If the preaching is offered in the same vernacular, no outsider coming in has any hope of understanding what is meant.

So much then for the commonest errors of preachers in the matter of style. Not one of us, I suppose, can hope to be completely blameless on every one of these counts. I have on occasion been guilty of them all. But to recognize where the dangerous shoals lie is something, and there is plenty of deep water between. If style is personality in writing and speaking, one can heed these warnings and still not feel confined in expression. A Canaanitish vocabulary and an unctuous manner have done much to widen the gulf between the pulpit and the street. Most of us when we are guilty are unconscious of it ourselves, employing one vocabulary and tone for daily life and another for the conduct of worship. The difference between them was brought home to the people of St. Louis with startling suddenness awhile ago. A fervent religious service came to its crashing close, vocabulary and intonation both being in the manner felt to be fitting for the "Pulpit of the Air." Indeed, the unctuous overtones still hung on the atmosphere when the minister (unaware that he had not been cut off) was heard to remark in a natural but jubilant tone to his companions in the studio: "Well, boys, we hit it right on the nose that time."

5

MAKE IT PRACTICAL

So much preaching ends in the air. The people do not know what the preacher was after and sometimes doubt if the preacher himself knows. The sermon concludes and the congregation disperses, but with no clear idea what has to be done about the topic the preacher had discussed.

I

Know what you are after!

How does it happen that this vagueness hangs over the conclusion of many sermons and leaves the people with no practical tasks to be performed?

1. In some instances, no doubt, for the reason the people themselves suspect—because the message has not been thoroughly thought out; because it has not aimed to do one clear thing; because the structure was not taut, and clear, and firm; because the end was not clearly in view from the start; because in preparation the preacher gave a disproportionate amount of time to the

earlier part of the sermon and was driven to scamp his conclusion.

All this amounts to saying that he himself did not really know what he was after, and how then could he make the people know? The suspicions of the people were well founded. They did not know the practical conclusions because *he* did not know them. The man who aims at nothing in particular will hit it every time.

2. In other instances the preacher *does* know what he is after—but in a vague way. He is certain that "all problems are solved in Christ" and that an "outpouring of the Holy Spirit is our great need" and that "we have to go forward and upward." But what do those phrases amount to when honestly examined in the keen mind of a businessman? In his heart the businessman says: "So what?"

If Christ is the answer, how does he work in this present practical world? If we need an outpouring of the Holy Spirit, what are the plain conditions laid down in the Bible by which he may come in power? If we have to go forward and upward, may we know precisely what it is that we have to go forward and upward *to*— and *how*?

Discerning writers on homiletics have long known that the neglected word in preaching is the word "how." No amount of eloquence is a substitute for plainness in a conclusion. "If I speak with the tongues of men and of angels, but have not [*clarity*], I am become sounding brass, or a clanging cymbal."

It is a hard task as we shall see in a moment—and

harder with some types of sermons than others—but a preacher should steadily hold before himself the ambition of sending away all his hearers saying quietly to themselves: "This is what I have to do."

3. Still other sermons come to a vague conclusion, not because the preacher does not know what he is after and not because he could not put it into plain and practical terms if he wished, but because he is hindered by a disinclination to expose his heart in public on matters that are by their very nature private.

There is a healthy reticence in most men of spiritual sensitivity against displaying the secrets of their souls in public. They feel that their intercourse with God is a very personal thing. If a man has no close communion with God, well, he has nothing to hide, but if a man has a deep and secret devotional life, he may rightly fear to display spiritual pride, or claim an intimacy with God he does not possess, or pose as an expert on the spiritual life when he knows himself to be but a beginner.

All this is healthy and humble. But there is a kind of spiritual reticence which is not healthy and humble, and which can militate against the purposes of God in our lives. How loath Christian people are to talk to one another, for instance, about their methods in private prayer. How hesitant preachers are—even with their fellow preachers—to pass on any technique they have learned in aiding God to subdue the sin in their souls. They are all pilgrims from time to eternity with a serious responsibility to help one another to heaven, and yet this dumbness is common and men conceal the most important thing they know as though it were a guilty secret.

No wonder, then, that the silence extends to the pulpit as well, and many sermons are preached, for example, on the importance of prayer, or on the necessity of imitating Christ, or on the duty of outwitting temptation, or on the privilege of being filled with divine love, in which the *how* of it is barely touched. The more successful the sermon is in establishing the necessity of any of these important things, the more sharp is the disappointment of the congregation when it ends without the preacher getting down to ways and means. Every intelligent and heart-warmed hearer is saying in his heart: "How, Preacher? How? How do I learn to love prayer? How imitate my Lord? How outwit the devil? How open myself to the divine love? How?"

No man can answer those mute questions without drawing on his own spiritual experience. If he has little experience to draw upon, he may wonder how he became a preacher at all; but if (as is almost certainly the case) he has learned many things of his Lord through the years, he must overcome his shyness and tell it out.

He need not always put it into the first person. Much that he has learned he has found also in the practice of the saints (and may, indeed, have learned it from them), and he can step behind a great name as he sets it forth: "It was a custom of Fletcher of Madeley . . . ." "St. Teresa tells us . . . ." "In the journal of Henry Martyn . . . ." But his power to select the particular reference, and his glowing heart in telling it, will tell his people more than he knows. "Our minister knows that also," they will feel.

At other times he must be most plain: "I have found in my own life . . . ." So he exposes his heart and in fulfillment of his solemn responsibilities as the under-shepherd of the flock tells them all he knows, presses forward himself on the way to heaven, and beckons and enheartens them as he goes.

He cannot say everything he knows. No one—not even the saint—is able to put into plain words all the secret intercourse of God with his soul. But it is important to say, when God directs, as much as we can. It is not easy, but it is most necessary. The omission of these practical aids in preaching is a common and serious defect of the modern pulpit, and gives an "airy-fairy" conclusion to many sermons which should have come out sharp and clear and challenging.

Let a young preacher in his sermon preparation, especially when he is dealing with ethical sermons (holding up a virtue for emulation or denouncing some vice to his people's face)—let him pin up the word "how" in front of him, and let him count that sermon unfinished until he has wrought out in himself and in his prayer-thought with God all that he can say under that. "This is the way forward. . . ." "I suggest that you do this, and this. . . ."

Of such a man it may be confidently affirmed that, when his skill grows, his people will never disperse after worship saying in bewilderment: "How does he expect us to achieve all that?"

II

Doctrines must be preached practically and duties doctrinally

It will be said, however, by some who have followed me until now that certain sermons cannot possibly have a practical conclusion, and one must frankly admit that with some of them it is hard—doctrinal sermons, for instance, for which I made a special plea in Chap. 2. What practical conclusion, it may be asked, follows from a well-wrought sermon on the deity of Christ, or the doctrine of assurance, or the element of truth in predestination?

The word "practical" has not to be interpreted too narrowly. A new, healthy, positive way of *thinking* is a practical thing—in some circumstances the most practical thing of all.

But perhaps the most important thing to remember here is the dictum of the early Protestant theologians that doctrines must be preached practically and duties doctrinally.

It would be hard to exaggerate the deep wisdom of that dictum. The sad hiatus that has come between duties and doctrine explains many of the unhappy features of modern life. The absence of sound doctrine has reduced religion in the minds of many people to some vague sentimentalism which you can have or not have according to the fancy of the moment. God, if he can be said to exist in their minds at all, is an upright blur. Jesus is an archaic name, slightly embarrassing. Talk about the Holy Spirit is as unsubstantial to them as talk about spooks. Incarnation, atonement, and grace are meaningless counters they cannot intelligently exchange, and nothing in all this realm of ideas seems related to the duties of daily life.

Not understanding doctrine, these people have no real basis in reality for the duties of daily life. Morality is convention. If under duress they connect it with God at all, they do so with hesitation and confusion. If they have tried to think the matter through, they have concluded that "morals" are customs which people in time past have found socially convenient but which have no real and ultimate sanction. At a pinch they can be jettisoned. Tired of the same face over the breakfast table, you can go off with someone else. If what has proved socially convenient in time past proves now to be personally inconvenient, well—you need not be held by it. Nothing has eternal meaning. "What's right or wrong but thinking makes it so?" So think the way you like! Let changing desire be your erratic guide and recognize in your rare moments of lucidity that you are like a mariner lost on an uncharted ocean without a compass or a rudder.

To what a pass do people come who lose a firm grasp on doctrine and whose only basis for duty is that it is the "done thing"!

How clear it is, therefore, that doctrines and duties must be bound together, and how plain that the old dictum which required doctrines to be preached practically and duties doctrinally is deeply sound and urgently needs recovery. It holds together things which should never be put asunder. It shows duties rooted in the reality of God and doctrines underpinning the plain tasks of every day. Paul is our guide here as in so much else. Strong doctrine and plain morals are always tightly bound together by him. Ephesians and Colossians would both illustrate it. Clear Christology, a high doctrine of the Church, a strong warning against the current heresies—and it all issues at the last in "walk worthily." Be what you were meant to be. Live up to your new status. Sound doctrine shows you who and what you are. Let daily life confirm it!

What answer can be made to two married people involved in a guilty liaison and planning each to desert his loyal partner and advertise his incontinence and disloyalty to the world? They protest that they love each other, that their feelings for the one they promised "to love and to cherish till death do us part" have changed; they conceive of love as only emotion and not as a set will. What kind of argument is likely to prevail with them unless the fact of God, and the reality of God, and the will of God, have been built into their nature and unless they are made to feel that God forbids this deceitful thing and that the fiat of the Almighty is against it? What hope have we in an age of shameless theft, when many people have ceased to be sorry for stealing and are only sorry to be found out—what hope have we of making them honest in the dark unless we make God a reality to them and prove that the dif-

81

ference between "thine and mine" is embedded in his purposes and intended by him for all people through all time?

How clear it is, then, that an awful responsibility rests upon the preacher to bind together doctrine and duty, and how plain that the doctrines must be preached practically and the duties doctrinally. "If this dogma be true, plainly based and broadly set in the scriptures, does it not follow as an irresistible inference that we *ought* . . . ?" Or beginning with the duty, is not the preacher under the obligation of his divine calling not merely to exhort people to the moral imperative but to show them that it is a divine imperative too? The duty follows as a necessary inference from God's nature and his revealed will. So life takes wholeness. Human personality has meaning and eternal worth, human duties are buttressed by the commandments of the Lord of creation, and life has unity from the mighty God behind all things to a child struggling against the temptation to tell a lie.

But divorce those two, and there is chaos. Dogma becomes academic lumber—the dry-as-dust speculation of doctrinaires—and human duties are social conventions which we may accept or reject at our fancy; the ten commandments do not apply east of Suez and "scientifically" examined prove to be no more than outworn Jewish taboos! Immoral night descends upon the world, and losing grip on God, we are perilously near to losing grip on all things.

III

The importance of having no "morals"

How then can a preacher "earth" his message? He is transmitting the word from God, and it came to him through the Book, and through his prayer, and through his prayer-thought, and through the long experience of the Church. How can he show its day-to-day significance to men?

Let him work in the way I have suggested. When his sermon is mainly ethical in character, let him be careful to show how the high moral demand roots in the character and will of God; but when he is dealing with doctrine, or plain Bible exposition, or preaching a sermon I have classified as philosophic or apologetic, let him constantly hold before his mind the special responsibility to be as practical in his conclusions as he possibly can.

There is, perhaps, no need today to warn intelligent men against labored moralizing—"Now the lesson of all this . . . ," "The moral I want to draw out . . . ." [1] We can still recall the extra boredom which spread over us as children when the preacher got to that point. We recall also the little girl who said: "Our preacher is fine: he has no morals." Not many men are guilty today of those sententious "stuck-on" conclusions which signify that all interest is now over and only the heroic in the congregation can be expected to listen any more.

[1] Cf. *The Craft of Sermon Construction*, p. 138.

Moreover, this kind of moralizing is *not* the practical conclusion I am pleading for. It is usually a bit more theory and a lot more exhortation. In a practical conclusion a preacher aims at getting right into the context of his hearers' lives and showing them plain things they can do and clear things they can live on in their thinking. He is never afraid to be elementary, and he hates unnecessary vagueness as he hates the devil. He does not overface the people, putting upon them in any one sermon so many things to do that they cannot even remember them, much less feel exhilarated in translating them into life. The over-all impression the people should have is that their minister is living their life with them, sensing, and indeed experiencing, their own difficulties and sharing with them his discoveries on the road to holiness. He shows them what helps he has found in avoiding mind wandering in prayer, how they may learn to love people they do not like, how to hold the children to religion when they enter their difficult teens, how to cling to God in great trouble when all things cave in, how to walk by the little light of duty when the thrill and joy of the Christian adventure fade for a while from the mind.

Now and then, no doubt, the minister may soar above the heads of his average hearer. The rapture of religion will carry him away, and he will come near to saying things which, as the apostle Paul said, it is not lawful for a man to utter.

His people will allow him that. The more spiritually

mature among them will follow his flight, and he will remember that the most advanced of all have outflown *him*. But he will not soar away from his people every week. A leader who leads so far ahead that he passes out of vision no longer leads.

The normal sermon will end with down-to-earth practical things for the people to do, and those who are serious in the pursuit of holiness will know the next steps they have to take.

6

GLOW OVER IT

Some preaching fails in power because it fails in passion. It may be intellectually respectable, the points the sermon sets out to make may be well made and worth making, but there is no glow about it. The people depart, but they are inwardly unmoved, and they are unmoved because the preacher himself was unmoved. No one can carry conviction to others who is not filled with conviction himself.

But our feelings are not the servants of our will. Because passion adds something necessary to preaching, no man can say: "I'll put that right; I will have feeling." To resolve on such a course and act on the resolution leads one to the only kind of hypocrisy which is not rare among preachers.

I

The hypocrisy of faked feeling

The sort of hypocrite who proclaims in the pulpit what he inwardly disbelieves is almost unknown. The hardness of the life and the meager material returns make the ministry an unattractive calling to a man who wants paying in the cash of this world. But the milder hypocrisy of faked feelings is not uncommon in the pulpit, and it arises in this way: men recognize that preaching fails in power if it fails in passion, and when the feeling does not arise of itself, some of them put it on. They put it on sometimes so suddenly and sharply —beginning to shout or affecting a frenzy—that the hearers almost suspect a reminder on their notes that this is the point to apply the heat; and because hypocrisy in any form—even a form as mild as this—is abhorrent to a normal man, something of unreality steals over the whole exposition, and the hearers are not merely unmoved but embarrassed and repelled. Howsoever that passion which is part of the secret of power in preaching is recovered, it must be honestly recovered and not counterfeited. The glow must be the outward radiance of some burning light within.

Occasionally one hears in the pulpit a man who says nothing as though it were something. An organ voice and a grand manner give a spurious air of profundity to his unimportant thoughts. Announcing and repeating his text as "He that worketh not," a preacher of this type went on immediately to say, "Hear how the great Dr. Agar Beet translates this passage: 'He that does not work. . . .'" A man who was present said that the absurdity of it all seemed quite concealed from most of the congregation by the sonorous tones in which it was uttered and by the preacher's obvious assurance that his variant translation had added immeasurably to the sense. But the ribald youths in the gallery would not have been deceived, and in their minds they would have satirically awarded the preacher a "bar to his D.D." for this further example of how to say nothing as though it were something.

Yet while it is a fact that some men can say nothing as though it were something, it is a much more common error among modern preachers to say something as though it were nothing. A man preaches on the Incarnation, but no hint of adoring wonder streams from the pulpit to the pew. If he is inwardly amazed himself at the incredible truth he is announcing, he is highly skillful in concealing it. He is asking people to believe that

> Being's source begins to be,
> And God himself is born!

but he might be giving a mild weather forecast. There is no wonder in him, and it is no wonder that there is no wonder in the pew.

Or he is preaching on the Cross and telling the people that this piteous figure staggering toward Golgotha and stained with the blood of the Garden and the pillar is none other than the Son of God consummating his sufferings for the sins of the whole world. The story may be told with a wealth of Bible references and a theological carefulness which leaves the congregation in no doubt that the preacher has put a lot into it.

But the absence of feeling robs it of power. They are aware that it is all familiar to him and trite by familiarity. His closest hearers feel within their hearts that he has put everything into it but himself, and the message which should have knocked them dumb with wonder seems to shrink to the level of a superior fairy tale. A man who is not moved himself has little hope of moving others.

Not that it must be inferred from this that deep feeling will express itself alike in every man. Temperament plays its part here. At the point when one man declaims and gesticulates and uses the whole range of his voice (naturally and convincingly), another stands motionless, his voice almost a quiet monotone but a white heat burning at the heart of all he says. A communication of passion comes over either way. While each is natural, no unreality can creep in.

One of the last public speeches of William Temple was made in the Westminster Central Hall. More than three thousand people hung on his words, and the speech was broadcast too. Press photographers continued to snap him throughout his address. Standing quite still, without a gesture and without a note, he unwound the sinuous argument which burned from time to time with a terrible intensity.

In pleading for passion in preaching, one does not plead for declamation, gesticulation, or even a raised voice. Let a man be himself, and most himself when he is carried away from himself. Let the feeling show itself how it will; but if there is no feeling, the preaching

89

will fail in conviction and all the preacher's words be lost on the wind.

II

How passion comes into preaching

But how does passion come into preaching? We have seen that to fake it savors of hypocrisy and that it must arise of itself in a man's mind and heart. How does it arise? By what mental or spiritual discipline can a man ensure that his words will have heat when they come to the people and arrest even the indifferent by their force and by their fervor?

1. Prayer is the chief way.

The powerful Negro preacher who said that in his preparation for the pulpit he "read himself full" and "thought himself clear" said also that he "prayed himself hot." The paramount part of prayer in preaching we have yet to consider, but we may remember in passing that Thomas Chalmers laid it down that the reason why ministers fail is not that they do not study, or do not preach, or do not visit, but that they do not pray. He added that we look on prayer as the means whereby we obtain all good things from God, and God looks upon prayer as the means whereby he is able to vitalize our nature at the roots. Out of that vitalizing at the roots of a preacher's life, passion enters his preaching.

2. Anything which deepens a preacher's faith in preaching adds to his passion in preaching the Word.

We noticed in Chap. 1 a number of things which deepen a man's faith in preaching. It has changed lives, changed towns, changed countries, and to some extent has changed the world. Most people who have put themselves under the proclamation of the gospel know that preaching has done mighty things for them —blasted doubt, nourished faith, communicated comfort, imparted strength.

Let a preacher dwell on these things as he prepares his sermon and prepares himself. Let him hold steadily in mind that through the medium of this sermon the Holy Spirit may work a miracle of transformation in someone's life, and the thought of it and the hope of it will kindle him with expectation. He is surely an unusual preacher who with any length of direct preaching does not know of someone transformed by the Spirit of God under the word as he gave it. Let him keep that transformed person clearly in mind. "God did that through so poor a tool as I. God could do that again. Lord! Lord!"

3. Anything which militates against familiarity in handling the word will also help to keep the glow in preaching.

It is almost blasphemous to say it, but the holiest things are not exempt from the law that familiarity breeds contempt. At least if it does not breed contempt, it robs them as they grow familiar of awe and rapture. This familiarity is one of the occupational diseases of the ministry, and a man must guard against it like a sane miner guards against pneumonoconiosis.

He must read his Bible not only for texts to preach on but for truth to live on.

He must sit away from his subject at times and recover again the rapture he first knew when religion really came alive to him.

He must recall how gloriously matched is the Christian gospel to human need, and imagine it impinging for the first time on the mind of a man to whom it had all been strange. By sanctified imagination he can live it all over again.

He must remind himself, when all his preparation is over and his foot is on the pulpit stair, that this particular theme (now half familiar because of the hours he has been working on it) will fall with freshness on his people's ears. *They* have not been moiling at it for hours. But *he* must feel its freshness again and give it with the dew upon it. It was said of Joseph Parker that *he* listened when he preached. He was not only the preacher but one of the congregation. He himself seemed surprised at the thoughts as he flung them out, and took them to himself as though they were especially intended for him. His congregation gained something from that. A preacher aware of the freshness and divine origin of what he is saying communicates his surprise and gratitude to the congregation too.

Whatever keeps wonder in a preacher's personal religion will keep wonder in his pulpit. Brooding on Charles Wesley's hymns is one way to it.

Where shall my wondering soul begin?
How shall I all to heaven aspire?

And can it be that I should gain
An interest in the Saviour's blood?

The speechless awe that dares not move,
And all the silent heaven of love.

4. The wind bloweth where it listeth, and we cannot make it blow; but we can learn of those areas where it blows most steadily—and we can put up our sail.

The sublime moments of the religious life are usually those moments in which a man realizes emotionally what he may have long known with the mind. It is impossible to believe that a trained theologian like John Wesley did not understand the doctrines of justification by faith and the new birth until Peter Böhler explained them to him. He understood the theory of it all right, but on May 24, 1738, the truth of his mind became a truth of his feelings. His heart was warmed, and the revival had begun.

Now that is a ministry of the Holy Spirit. He is constantly seeking to make real to those whose religion is a formality the secret rapturous wonder of it all. Nor must we suppose that the blowings of the Spirit are so uncertain as to partake of vagary. Anyone who studies the workings of the Holy Spirit, or who would inform himself of them, can know, as it were, the areas and seasons of the Spirit's blowing and be ready to hoist his sail when the wind of heaven comes.

I am writing this in a ship off the coast of Portugal. I can clearly see the heights of Torres Vedras. Over those mountains at certain seasons blow the strong winds known as the Portuguese Trades. Mariners have known them for centuries. Time was when vessels bound for the East (and West) gathered here in great armadas, and as those strong and steady winds blew out on the wide ocean, up went the sails of the waiting vessels and over the sea went the ships.

The wind bloweth where it listeth. True! and so does the Spirit of God. But neither is of caprice, and neither is utterly unpredictable.

Let any man eager to feel again (or for the first time) the afflatus of divine power in his preaching study all that can be known of the winds of the Spirit; let him be in the areas of his blowing and let him hoist his sail.

To this simple strategy sincerely followed, God will not deny his servant's desire. Prayer will warm him. Recalling the past effectiveness of preaching, conviction will deepen in him. Wonder kept fresh will hold that stale familiarity at bay. The Holy Spirit will breathe upon him, and his preaching will be powerful for God.

Then will he love his work, and there will be a glow and a joy in his preaching which will communicate itself to his hearers as well.

Said Samuel Chadwick:

I like to see a workman step back and look at his job. No eight-hour day for me! I have not worked as wisely or as well as I might, but the only dull days I have had are those when there was nothing I could do. If there is one person in the world I pity, it is the one who has had no love for his job. What a drudgery. I have loved mine with a passionate and consuming love. I would rather preach than do anything else I know in this world. I have never missed a chance to preach. I would rather preach than eat my dinner, or have a holiday, or anything else the world can offer. I would rather pay to preach, than be paid not to preach. It has its price in agony of sweat and tears and no calling has such joys and heart-breaks, but it is a calling an archangel might covet; and I thank God that of His grace He called me into His ministry. Is there any joy like that of saving a soul from death? Any thrill like that of opening blind eyes? Any reward like the love of little children to the second and third generation? Any treasure like the grateful love of hearts healed and comforted? I tell you it is a glorious privilege to share the travail and the wine of God. I wish I had been a better minister, but there is nothing in God's world or worlds I would rather be.[1]

[1] Norman G. Dunning, *Samuel Chadwick,* p. 17.

7

STEEP IT IN PRAYER

To say, finally, that no preaching is powerful which is not steeped in prayer is not to utter a pious afterthought. It is so true and so much the heart of all the truth on this subject that if we had but one thing to say in place of seven, it would be this. No amount of labor, no amount of labor on central things, no effort to make preaching plain and practical, no study to learn how to glow over it and grow in faith in its importance, would have any sense in itself or hope of success if the preaching were not all drenched in devotion. The man who would toss this plea aside on the ground that he knows it already probably does not know it at all. The man who really "knows it already" is never loath to be reminded again.

All Christian preaching must be steeped in prayer.

1. The very nature of preaching requires it.[1]
Christian preaching, as I do not weary of insisting, is the

---

[1] Cf. prayer-thought, pp. 56-58, above.

proclamation of a message from God. It is not a human address; it is a divine pronouncement. A pulpit and a platform are not the same thing. If there are occasions —and there will be—when the preacher has no direct word from God but wants to offer an opinion of his own, he may do so, but (like the apostle Paul) he will not confuse the two, and normally he will make the distinction clear to his hearers.

The preacher—as preacher—is a herald. He is not offering his own comments on life and events. Thoughts which are entirely his own thoughts (be they deep or shallow) he will express as his will and the occasion requires, but as a preacher he announces the mighty acts and purposes of God. He tells men things they could not know by their own thinking—that God is love, that he came to earth in the flesh, that he is merciful and gracious, that he "receiveth sinful men."

Every herald must know his monarch's mind. How else can he proclaim it? And he knows it not only by the Book but by his own personal commerce with the One he represents. He knows him in prayer, and the better he knows him, the more he has to tell. Clearly the very nature of preaching requires that it be begotten in large part by prayer.

2. Every part of preaching requires it.
It is not uncommon among preachers to work hard at their message and, when it is ready to be delivered, to add a prayer that its use may be attended with blessing.

The prayer is offered like a little flavoring to a dish already made.

But that is not to *steep* preaching in prayer. The praying that affects preaching is the praying that has saturated its every part. It is not something added at the end or put in as a spice as we go, but something which so much belongs to the substance and the nature and the shape of the finished thing that its absence would make it completely something else. From beginning to end preaching must be impregnated with prayer.

A sermon may begin in a preacher's mind in various ways. It may start as a thought or as a text. Some facet of divine truth may gleam with extra brightness in the preacher's mind or some fragment of the Book of God glow with a new light. There is a sense of "givenness" about it either way. The praying preacher instantly recognizes its origin and holds it out for further blessing from its divine source. His first grateful regarding of this freshly seen gleam of truth is all in the light of God. If the thought or the text must be noted but set aside for the time being, both are done in prayer.

How long the subject is left aside depends on many things. A subject may demand to be dealt with immediately or invite a period of quiet maturing. Some preachers regard these treasured and "given" seed thoughts as so many cuttings in a greenhouse, and they visit them to water them and watch them grow.

All the watering is done by the wise in prayer. They see the theme all the time as from the angle of God.

"What God wants to do with it" is their whole concern —not how original they can be, or what they can say that nobody has said before, or how startling, or how fresh—but what God wants to do with it. This steady and early regarding of the theme secures them from the snares of their own cleverness and fixes their single eye on the sole glory of God.

When the time comes for seriously taking the theme in hand, they go to work again with God. The actual fixing and limiting of the area to be covered is (as we have seen) the fruit of prayer thought; the treatment, and the divisions, and the predetermined conclusion, are all worked out in prayer. It is in the atmosphere and, indeed, in the constant practice of prayer that the illustrations are sought and fixed, and the appeal is shaped. The actual delivery comes from a mind and heart whose native air is prayer. When the sermon ends, the prayer continues. Of such a sermon it could never truly be said that it has "gone with the wind." It echoes in the memory of those who heard it, and it echoes the louder because the preacher is following his pleadings with his prayers.

No preaching can be really powerful for God in which prayer is only an afterthought. Every part of it must be made in prayer. The warp and the woof must both belong to devotion.

3. Each element of powerful preaching already distinguished in these lectures requires it.
Prayer is the single sovereign way of securing all I

have pleaded for in these chapters. The man who prays much in his preaching will keep to *centralities*. He must! The compass of his prayers will keep him on a true course. The temptation to wander off into marginal things will be resisted by his prime concern. He wants to proclaim the grace and favor of God. He wants to display his "mercy's whole design." How then can he become entangled with the frills of things? The smart novelties which drew him at one time seem little more than wisecracks now. The being and the love and the forgiveness of God fill his adoring mind and heart. Bethlehem, Nazareth, Calvary, and Olivet quicken his imagination and suggest a hundred varied themes. When the problems of this world keep him in London, Boston, Sydney, or Delhi, his preaching is still God-centered preaching because he is a God-centered preacher. Prayer with him is the prime business of every day, and he keeps to centralities without effort and without fail.

Nor can a man so devout, and so sure that it pleases God still by the foolishness of preaching to save them that believe, fail to *work* at his message. The childish idea that prayer is a substitute for work amuses him. He knows that some things come by prayer and cannot come by work, but he does not see work and prayer in rivalry. Work without prayer, he has found, produces clever ineffectiveness. Prayer without work has not been wholly sterile of spiritual gain, but he has come to realize that it is not a maximum for God. In work and prayer together he has found the blessing of the Lord resting most richly upon him.

If the bias of his nature—as with most modern preachers—is to work more rather than to pray more, he will drag himself to his knees rather than miss his appointments with God. If he believed once that prayer is acceptable only when one feels like praying, he believes that no longer. Without the aid of feeling, indeed sometimes in a sheer head-on conflict with feeling, he will have fellowship with the Father, who can make more of our prayers offered without feeling than of those which rise easily because they rise of desire. And from those prayers he turns to his work with renewed earnestness and works the harder because he has prayed the more.

Nor can a praying preacher fail for long in making the message *plain*. The subtle desire to appear clever is seen as pride and vanity when it is seen in the light of prayer. The praying preacher, held by his prayers to central things, has a great longing that his Master's message be understood.

There have been heralds who have made their proclamation as indistinctly as some town criers have made theirs and left one wondering how they got the appointment. But the preacher who prays much knows that he must make his message plain. He remembers Denney's word that a preacher cannot give at the same time the impression that he is clever and that Jesus is wonderful. He wants Jesus to be seen as wonderful. He longs to efface himself. He does not hunger for praise when the preaching is over. He wants sinners converted, be-

lievers strengthened, backsliders recovered, the sorrow-
ful comforted. Therefore he must be plain. At all costs
he must be plain. Praying as he prepares to preach, he
hears his Father's clear interrogation: "Is it plain?"

Time was perhaps when his love of homiletics tricked
him into delight at his own subtlety and gave him a
craftsman's joy at a dexterous use of points and counter-
points—but that is past now. Preaching as a dying man
to dying men, his great concern is to open up the rich
treasures of the gospel and to state it in such a way that
all but the feeble-minded can take it in. And it is prayer
that has made him eager to make it plain. At the last
the secret of power in preaching is to have power in
prayer.

It is by prayer that a preacher's desire to be *practical*
is kept clear before his eyes. The man who prays much
about his preaching does not see preaching as an art—
something that can be delighted in for itself alone. He
knows that God intends that it should *do* something—
something memorable and mighty. The idea of a sermon
as a graceful little essay, interlarded with reasonably
apt literary allusions and displaying the width of the
preacher's reading rather than the whole counsel of God,
is a concept of preaching from which he now recoils. If
a praying preacher thinks of himself in this connection
at all, he thinks, not of the impression that he is making
personally on the people's minds, but of the practical
outcome of that impression. What is the end of it all?
When his preaching days are over and he has time in the
evening of life to sit a little by the fire, will it be any

comfort that people praised him?—that crowds came?—
that he was said to be "influential"?—that he was a
popular preacher? Will not the important questions
then seem: "What lives were changed? What penitents
found forgiveness? What wavering souls were strengthened? What brokenhearted learned to hope again?
What—by the grace of God—did my preaching *do* in
people's lives? How clear did I make it that for every
Christian on every day of his life there is another step,
and what success did I have in indicating the step that
it might be?"

It is a secret prayer which keeps questions like these
foremost in a preacher's mind, the prayer unmarked of
men but known to God, the prayer by which its very
privacy can bring no adulation from other people but
which orientates the whole life to its divine Lord.

Warmth comes into preaching the same way. No truly
advanced soul prays just because of the consequences of
praying. The more mature we become, the more we pray
just to have fellowship with God and for God to use the
fellowship how he will. But because it *is* fellowship with
God, the most glorious consequences flow from it and
necessarily affect the whole orderings of life. The consequences are most pronounced in a preacher. To his
ungrudging toil at central things, and the ability to make
his message both plain and practical, is added this in-
terior glow, and his meaning is conveyed not only by the
medium of clear truth but with heart power as well.

The inertia of nature, the impediments of sin, the
fatal ease with which we can get used to things, the self-

ishness which robs us so easily of concern over others, have all to be overcome if a preacher is to burn consistently with holy zeal. God stirs the fire as the preacher prays. In prayer the preacher draws nearer to the burning heart of God, and his own heart burns the nearer he comes. An icicle has no future near a glowing fire. The coldness which creeps upon the preacher at times, his carelessness about the spiritual destiny of others, his dreadful familiarity with holy things, his loss of rapture and his loss of wonder, too, are only successfully overcome this way.

"Feelings do not matter," we often say, and if the absence of feeling is being used as an excuse for the absence of prayer, we say so truly. But feeling *does* matter in the pulpit. The profoundest truths uttered without feeling and without obvious conviction will have little effect on any congregation. To any preacher, therefore, consciously cold at the prospect of proclaiming the eternal gospel, we can only say: "Pray yourself hot." And if he answers that even in so holy an occupation prayer must not be used as though it were just a means to an end, we will simply say "Pray," and God can be trusted to do the rest.

Sometimes he does it suddenly. The preacher begins almost with a chill at his heart. He is stating the divine facts as he knows them and in a matter-of-fact way. Suddenly the sermon takes fire. Some view of the Cross, some wave of new wonder, some blessed dividend paid on prayers faithfully offered when feeling was all at ebb, breaks on the preacher; the words surge from his mouth and his heart at the same time. The congregation is held, gripped, subdued, awed, melted. The people steal away when the service is over knowing that they have been under the word of the Lord.

Is it any wonder that the gospel faithfully proclaimed, thought out and wrought out, plain and practical, and offered with passion because it was conceived and brought forth and nurtured in prayer, should be easy to believe in? It does the work. It carries its own authority with it. It would be harder to disbelieve it than to believe it. Faith in the gospel and faith in preaching as the prime means of its proclamation fill the preacher's mind, and he gives himself to it as a man who knows that he was called of God.

4. A holy life requires it.

Prayer is the secret of a holy life. Reduced to its minimum, the way of sanctity centers in two words: *attend* and *obey*. The saints of all communions come by grace to their serene and un-self-conscious distinction by the same means: they attend to God and they obey his word.

Prayer is the means by which they attend to God. They "talk oft with their Lord." They love his fellowship. Communion with him is the framework of all their days. All their "work" is done in intervals, the intervals of their prayers. Prayer is so much a part of their life that they do literally "pray without ceasing." When their mind is necessarily given to mundane things, they are still on the knees of their soul. Released from business

105

cares, their whole mind and heart revert to their Lord as by some homing instinct. With passing years even their wandering thoughts wander to him. Holiness is the fruit, first, of their prayers.

Holiness is the secret of unction. Unction is that mystic plus in preaching which no one can define and no one (with any spiritual sensitivity at all) can mistake. Men have it, or they do not have it. It is a thing apart from good sermon outlines, helpful spiritual insights, wise understanding, or eloquent speech. It can use all these media—and dispense with them. It is rare, indefinable, and unspeakably precious.

One of the things which distinguishes preaching from all other forms of public address is that preaching can have unction. That it has it so rarely is the shame of us preachers and proves the poverty of our prayers.

In all our ignorance of unction one thing at least is clear. It comes only of praying. It is the extra expression in a preacher of a holy life. It cannot be studied in separation any more than an aura can be studied apart from the light which reflects it. It is the clearest proof that the King indwells the herald he has sent to proclaim his word.

Unction can never be faked. Men have tried to counterfeit it and have produced unctuousness from which the soul of any normal man recoils as from hypocrisy. Divine in its origin, the true thing always bears the divine seal.

Preaching that has unction is preaching apart. Not all the craft of homiletics can make up for its absence.

Even the simplest word with unction has power to convey the felt presence of God.

Unction comes only of praying. Other things precious to a preacher come of prayer *and* something else. Unction comes only of praying. If nothing else revealed the poverty of our secret prayers, the absence of unction would. Able preaching can often reveal the cleverness of a man. "What clear distinctions! What dexterous use of words! What telling illustrations!" Unction reveals the presence of God.

Normally men with unction are as unaware of it as a saint is unaware of his sanctity. Such a preacher may feel on occasion that "God made free use of him." He may be vaguely aware that what he said was somehow not his own; it was all given; he was spoken *through*. A nimbus will rest on that preacher, and people will say in their own words: "Glory shone around!"

Prayer is the way—secret prayer, more prayer, much prayer. The last and greatest thing to say of power in preaching is that preacher and preaching must be steeped in prayer.

INDEX OF NAMES